LEATHERNECK

Molding Recruit Maggots into U.S. Marines in the 1950s

Darrell J. Ahrens
Corporal USMC
Lt. Colonel USAF (Ret)

© Copyright 2024 Darrell J. Ahrens

All rights reserved. No part of this book may be reproduced in any form or by any electronic or mechanical means, including information storage and retrieval systems, without written permission from the author, except in the case of a reviewer, who may quote brief passages embodied in critical articles or in a review.

Trademarked names may appear throughout this book. Rather than use a trademark symbol with every occurrence of a trademarked name, names are used in an editorial fashion, with no intention of infringement of the respective owner's trademark.

The information in this book is distributed on an "as is" basis, without warranty. Although every precaution has been taken in the preparation of this work, neither the author nor the publisher shall have any liability to any person or entity with respect to any loss or damage caused or alleged to be caused directly or indirectly by the information contained in this book.

Cover Design by Tatiana Fernandez
Interior Formatting by Brian Schwartz

v24-1216

Other books by Darrell Ahrens
Available at Amazon and other book outlets

Perspectives on the word "Tolerance," its corruption by radical liberal progressives, and the corrosive effects on Religion, Government, Education, and Culture

Memories and Confessions of a Fighter Pilot

Exposing the new Radicalized Democrat Party

Practical Theology for the Abundant Life Jesus promised

Table of Contents

Explanation of Title and Narrative Symbology 7
The Marine Corps Hymn 9
Foreword 10
Introduction 15
Chapter 1 - An Explosive Greeting 17
Chapter 2 - In-Processing 19
Chapter 3 - The Drill Instructors 27
Chapter 4 - Rules for Recruits 31
Chapter 5 - The Marine's Companion 37
Chapter 6 - To the Last Man 39
Chapter 7 - No Favoritism 41
Chapter 8 - Tragedy at Parris Island 43
Chapter 9 - The Smoking Lamp 45
Chapter 10 - Initial Training 47
Chapter 11 - The Marine Guard 57
Chapter 12 - First-Aid Classes 61
Chapter 13 - Physical Training 69
Chapter 14 - Camp Matthews Rifle Range (Part 1) 77
Chapter 15 - Camp Matthews Rifle Range (Part 2) 83
Chapter 16 - Water Survival 115
Chapter 17 - Gas Chamber 123
Chapter 18 - Bayonet Training 133
Chapter 19 - The Light at The End of The Tunnel 147
Chapter 20 - Graduation 153
Postscript 165
Addendum 171

"Some people spend an entire lifetime wondering if they made a difference in this world. Marines don't have that problem."

President Ronald Reagan

Explanation of Title and Narrative Symbology

The Sub-title *Molding Recruit Maggots into U.S. Marines in the 1950s* refers to the progression of a recruit to a full-fledged United States Marine. Obviously, the individual begins as a civilian recruit. The recruit is then identified as a maggot, a favorite name among the Drill Instructors' many insulting, demeaning, and profane names for the trainees. As maggots, they are associated with the lowest form of life, and reminded that the Drill Instructors' job is to transform them into what they considered the highest form of life - a United States Marine. The Drill Instructors would do this by breaking the recruits down into total submission, and then rebuild them with confidence, discipline, loyalty, honor, and toughness into one of the few, the proud, a Marine.

To present Marine Corps boot camp in the 1950s in all its reality, the pages of this book would be littered with gross, imaginative, and colorful profanity. I have chosen not to do that. However, where reference to profanity is necessary to emphasize a statement or action, I have used the literary symbols for profanity to indicate such instead of the words. As an aside, the excessive use of profanity, common in Marine boot camp in the '50s, has apparently long been discontinued as I discovered years ago, when I visited the Marine Corps Recruit Depot at San Diego and observed Drill Instructors drilling their platoons on the parade field. I heard no profanity. Marine Corps boot camp is still, without a doubt, the longest and absolute toughest boot camp of all the services, and yes, even what some might consider somewhat brutal at times, but the language has apparently been cleaned up.

The pictures and photos referred to in the narrative for each chapter are shown at the end of each chapter and are identified by the number referred to in the narrative.

> NOTE: The illustrations and pictures contained in this book are taken primarily from the following two sources:
> 1. My personal copy of the "Guidebook for Marines," Copyright 1956 by The Leatherneck Association, Inc. There are no restrictions concerning the copyright noted in this Guidebook.
> 2. My personal copy of our ***Platoon Yearbook*** made available to us on graduation from boot camp. There is no copyright designated for this yearbook.

*"To observe a Marine is inspirational.
To be a Marine is exceptional."*

Gunnery Sgt. Charles F. Wolf Jr.

The Marine Corps Hymn

From the Halls of Montezuma,
to the shores of Tripoli;
We fight our country's battles
in the air, on land, and sea.
First to fight for right and freedom,
and to keep our honor clean;
We are proud to claim the title
of United States Marine.

Our flags unfurled to every breeze,
from dawn to setting sun;
We have fought in every clime and place
where we could take a gun;
In the snow of far off northern lands,
and in sunny tropic scenes;
You will find us always on the job -
The United States Marine

Here's health to you and to our Corps,
which we are proud to serve;
In many a strife we've fought for life,
and never lost our nerve.
If the Army and the Navy
ever look on heaven's scenes,
They will find the streets are guarded
by United States Marines.

"For over 221 years, our Corps has done two things for this great nation; we make Marines and we win battles."

Gen. Charles C. Krulak
Commandant, USMC, May 5, 1997

Foreword

The United States Marine Corps came into existence to support naval forces in the Revolutionary War. It was established on November 10, 1775, by the Second Continental Congress meeting in Philadelphia, Pennsylvania. The recruiting headquarters was set up in the Tun Tavern on water street in Philadelphia, which is considered to be the birthplace of the Marine Corps. Marines consider it appropriate and are proud of the fact that the birthplace of the Corps was in a tavern.

The Marine Corps, perhaps even more than the other services, has developed many traditions, and over the years many generations of Marines have maintained, perpetuated, and honored those traditions. The familiar emblem of globe and anchor, adopted in 1868, embodies the history of world-wide service and sea traditions. The eagle, symbol of the nation itself, holds in its beak a streamer upon which is inscribed the famous motto of the United States Marines: Semper Fidelis, which in Latin means, "Always Faithful!"

The famous blue uniform of the Marine Corps, which is the envy of the other military branches, was first authorized by Secretary of War James McHenry on August 24, 1797, and incorporates many of the traditions of the Corps. The color blue represents the color of the sea and the primary mission of the Marine Corps as sea-going infantry. The pattern and trimmings of red and gold serves to make the uniform distinctive; however, the red edging or piping on the blouse serves as a reminder that John Paul Jones, the first Chief of Naval Operations during the Revolutionary War, dressed his Marines in red uniforms. Although no historical reason is given for the red stripe on the outer seams of the trousers worn by officers and non-commissioned officers of the Corps, which were adopted shortly after the Mexican War, tradition has it that the red stripes commemorate the bloody battle of Chapultepec.

In view of the fact that the early organization, duties, and regulations of the U.S. Marines were patterned somewhat after the ways and customs of their forerunners, the British Marines, it is possible that the traditional red of the British uniform had its effect on the adoption of red for the uniform of the American Marines.

The term "Leatherneck," as applied to Marines, is widely used, but few people associate it with the uniform. The fact that Marines wore a black leather collar from 1798 to 1880 may have given rise to the name. According to tradition, the collar was originally worn to protect the jugular vein from the slash of a saber or cutlass.

The sword, with a mameluke hilt, presented to Lieutenant Presley N. O'Bannon of the Marine Corps by a former Pasha of Tripoli, became the symbol of authority of Marine Corps officers for more than 100 years. The exploits of Lieutenant O'Bannon and his Marines on the shores of Tripoli in 1805 became legend and were climaxed by the raising of the American flag for the first time in the Old World.

According to the "Guidebook for Marines," the handbook for recruits, military discipline is the state of order and obedience among military personnel resulting from training. Discipline in the Marine Corps does not refer to regulations, punishments, or a state of subservience. What is meant by discipline is the exact execution of orders, resulting from an intelligent, willing obedience, rather than an obedience based solely upon habit or fear.

Habit, however, does play its part, and for this reason, the Marines benefit from their emphasis on things as Rifle Drill, Close Order Drill, Formation Drill, Physical Drill which hone precision and discipline. Punishment of individuals for breaches of discipline can be harsh in the Corps, but only to reform the lax or eliminate those who are unfit, morally, mentally, or physically to serve in the Corps.

Discipline is necessary to secure orderly action which alone can triumph over the confusion and seemingly impossible conditions of battle. The individual must be able to recognize and face fear because fear is the enemy of discipline. Fear is natural, and controlled fear can be a powerful force, but fear unchecked will lead to panic, and a unit that panics is no longer a disciplined unit, but a mob. There is no sane person who is without fear, but with good discipline and high morale, all can face danger and overcome the fear.

When a Marine learns to be a disciplined warrior, he has learned a sense of obligation to himself and to his comrades, to his commander, and to the Marine Corps. He has learned that he is a member of a team which is organized, trained, and equipped for the purpose of engaging and defeating enemies of his country. The final objective of military discipline is effectiveness in combat - to make sure that a unit performs correctly in battle, that it performs its assigned mission, achieves its objectives, and helps others to achieve their objectives.

Marines must never forget that they carry the badge of their Corps and their country, and that those who see them regard them not as individuals, but as representatives of the Corps whose insignia they wear. If they appear tough, smart, alert, and efficient, others will not only say, "That is an outstanding Marine," but also, "Certainly he belongs to an outstanding unit." Developing the habit of prompt obedience to all orders will improve the discipline of each individual and the unit. It is too late to learn discipline on the battlefield. It must be learned in training, and that training emphasizes teamwork, so that the concept of "brothers in arms" takes shape and grows, so that they learn to have each other's back, learn to think and act alike which sharpens unit cohesion, and enables them, as a team, to accomplish increasingly difficult tasks in a manner in which they can take pride.

Along with military discipline, and inseparable from it, is military courtesy. This is expressed in many ways, always referring to officers as sir, addressing senior enlisted Marines by their rank, standing when a superior ranking Marine enters the room, and the most common act of courtesy - the salute. The salute figuratively expresses to the other person that he is your brother-in-arms, that he can count on you, and that you have his back.

The recruit's first introduction to this core of military discipline and courtesy, Marine style, is when he/she enters the gates of Marine Recruit Depot, San Diego, California or Parris Island, South Carolina. And it most certainly is an exceptionally frightening and rude introduction. My introduction to this Marine discipline and courtesy, and its effects on my 19-year-old body, mind, and spirit, are the contents of this book.

"There are only two kinds of people that understand Marines; Marines and the enemy. Everyone else has a second-hand opinion."

Gen. William Thornson
U.S. Army

Introduction

This book is an account of the longest 12 weeks of my life, 12 weeks of fear, pain, challenge, suffering, failure, insult, discipline, success, joy, accomplishment, and pride - in other words, 12 weeks of Marine Corps boot camp, the first step in establishing the legacy, "Once a Marine, always a Marine."

Marine Corps boot camp has always had the reputation of being the toughest basic training of all the services. I enlisted in the Marines when I was 18 years old, and left for boot camp on my 19th birthday, February 28, 1956. I submit that, in 1956, the word "tough" to describe Marine boot camp was woefully inadequate. "Brutal" would be a more apt term. Perhaps one of the reasons for this was because it had only been 11 years since the end of World War II and only 3 years since the Korean War ended, and memories were fresh. We had entered World War II woefully unprepared since we had decimated the size and readiness of the military after World War I on the assumption that the first world war had been a war to end all wars. Incredibly, we made the same mistake after World War II, and again drastically reduced the size and readiness of our military, resulting in our being, to a great extent, unprepared for the Korean War. I think the powers that be took the attitude, "Never again will we be unprepared," and this attitude translated to the military with a corresponding effect on the training. Add to this that it had become apparent that the Soviet Union was an enemy, and the nation would have to maintain a strong military in readiness.

As noted, the Marine Corps places great emphasis on tradition and takes great pride in their magnificent tradition. Even their hymn begins with reference to their tradition - "From the halls of Montezuma, to the shores of Tripoli…". When the other services, Army, Navy, Air Force, somewhat lowered the standards and demands of their basic training, along with the length of their boot camp from eight weeks to six weeks, the Marines would have none of it. To lower standards and length of boot camp to less than 12 weeks would be a violation of Marine tradition.

Why did I enlist in the Marines? Three reasons! First, I had just completed my third semester of college. I was doing well, getting good grades, but was bored with college life and wanted some excitement and adventure. One of my classmates felt the same, and we decided that joining the Marines would be an exciting and adventuress thing to do. He backed out at the last moment and joined the Navy while I held to our original plan.

Second, my boyhood dream was to be a fighter pilot, and I heard that the Marines needed pilots more than the other services and therefore the chances of getting an appointment to pilot training would be greater in the Marines.

And third, to prove myself. One of my cousins had been in the Marines during World War II, and had participated in the invasions of Tarawa, Saipan, and Okinawa, as I recall. A younger cousin was in the Marines at this time in 1956, along with the future husband of another cousin. I was a skinny kid weighing around 125 pounds, and when I once mentioned that I would like to join the Marines, a couple uncles and other relation told me that I wasn't physically capable of being a Marine. So, I decided to show them.

Marine recruits from the eastern part of the United States were sent to the Marine Recruit Depot at Parris Island, South Carolina, and Marine recruits from the middle west and western part of the United States were sent to the Marine Recruit Depot at San Diego, California. Being from Nebraska, I was sent to San Diego. And so, on the morning of February 28, 1956, I and a half dozen other recruits boarded a four-engine airliner in Omaha, Nebraska for our flight to San Diego. When I arrived in Omaha, I was surprised to discover that one of those recruits was a neighbor who was a former classmate of mine in high school and whose parents lived a block or so from mine. His name was John, and I will mention him in a subsequent chapter.

Before we left, the Marine recruiter appointed me as leader of the group, with the responsibility of keeping them together after our arrival at Lindberg Airport in San Diego and informing the Duty Officer at the Recruit Depot of our arrival. He gave me the phone number to call and change for a pay phone at the airport. The flight to San Diego was a special treat for me since it was my first flight in an aircraft, and as mentioned, I had pilot ambitions. The airliner was the Constellation, one of the most modern new designs, with four engines and triple vertical stabilizers.

Chapter 1
An Explosive Greeting

I am sure that I have the distinction of being the only Marine recruit to have received a royal ass-chewing from an unknown Drill Instructor before I even entered the gates of the Marine Recruit Depot. Here's how it happened. After we arrived at Lindberg Airport in San Diego, deplaned and got our luggage, which was only one duffel bag each, I gathered the recruits together and told them to remain in that area of the terminal and stay close while I phoned the Depot and informed them of our arrival. I soon learned that trying to herd that group of recruits was about as difficult as trying to herd a bunch of cats. They were all from Nebraska, the deep Midwest, and here they were in California, a mystical state in their minds. Few, if any of them, had ever been in an international airport, and here they were in San Diego's Lindberg International Airport. Naturally they wanted to walk around, explore their surroundings, and revel in the feeling that they were actually in California.

I took the note with the phone number and the change the recruiter in Omaha had given me and went to find a pay phone and make the call. After many rings, I finally got an answer, identified myself, and gave the reason for my call. I was told to keep the recruits together in the passenger lounge and a bus would be sent to pick us up. With a smart "Yes Sir!" I hung up.

Well, we waited, and waited, and waited some more. After more than an hour, I was wondering if they had forgotten about us, and whether I should make another call to remind them of our arrival. I decided to wait a bit longer. After another 30 minutes or so, I decided to make that call. Big, big, mistake. The voice that answered was the same voice that had answered before. I again identified myself as Private Ahrens and that I and a group of newly arrived recruits were at the airport. The voice asked, "Are you the recruit who called before?" I answered, "Yes Sir!" The voice asked, "And what did I tell you before?" I answered, "You told us to stay together, and you would send a bus to pick us up."

And then it happened! The phone line erupted into a very loud cascade of profanity and insult my 19-year-old ears had never heard the likes of before. "Well, you xx#zo!x#, I meant exactly what I said. Now, you get off this xx#zo!x# phone, get back to your fellow xx#zo!x# recruits, stay together in the xx#zo!x# passenger lounge, and wait until hell freezes over if necessary for the xx#zo!x# bus I will send. And stay away from the xx#zo!x# phone. Do I make myself xx#zo!x# clear?"

Instead of answering with a smart "Yes Sir!" this time, I responded with a panicked "Yes Sir!" "Yes Sir!" "Yes Sir!" Well, the bus finally arrived, and I remember hoping and praying that the Drill Instructor who owned that voice over the phone would not be among the Drill Instructors meeting the bus, and ask, "Which one of you made that phone call?" Thankfully, he wasn't.

> *"Bravery is being the only one who knows you're afraid."*
>
> — *USMC Quote, Unknown*

Chapter 2
In~Processing

> "If I charge, follow me. If I retreat, kill me.
> If I die, revenge me."
> USMC saying, Anonymous

As the bus entered the Marine Corps Recruit Depot in San Diego, we had a panoramic view of the base. I remember my first impression was of its beauty, the Spanish architecture of the buildings with their columns and arches, and the dominant centerpiece of the parade ground, the drill field, which as I recall, was two miles in circumference, and which we recruits would come to know intimately as the Grinder, since a major part of basic training was drill, drill, and more drill. Pictures 1 and 2 on the last page of this chapter give some indication of its beauty.

Our first stop was the receiving barracks, shown on picture 3, where we would spend the night since it was late afternoon when we arrived. A couple of non-commissioned officers met us, hustled us off the bus, took us into a room, and handed each of us a container with the instructions to deposit any drugs, food, drink, candy, gum, porno material, etc., in the container. We were told that nothing we put into that container would be held against us, so we need not fear retribution. However, any attempt to hide anything, or hold anything back, would be severely dealt with.

We were allowed to keep cigarettes and lighter; however, smoking was strictly forbidden except by permission of the assigned Drill Instructors, who would not come to take command of us until the next day. So, we smokers would have an extended period of non-smoking.

After a trip to the mess hall for dinner, or supper for us Midwesterners, it was back to the receiving barracks for the night. It had been a long day; we were exhausted and looking forward to a good night's sleep. How naive of us to expect that we would have such a blessing. We were shown where the duty officer's office was, and then taken to the sleeping quarters and each of us assigned a bunk.

After we were in bed, it wasn't long before the shouts resounded: "Recruit maggot (insert name), report to the duty station!" Upon jumping out of bed, running to the duty station and reporting to the duty officer, the recruit was greeted with insult and a chewing out for taking so long to report, and a reminder that the recruit was to be there in a matter of seconds if not sooner. The recruit would then be assigned a chore by the duty officer.

When I, as recruit maggot Ahrens, got my first call to the duty station, and after a royal chewing out for taking too much time getting there, my first chore was to get the duty officer a cup of coffee, and it had better be to his perfection or punishment would follow. It soon became apparent to us that, whatever chore was given us by our duty officer, we would never accomplish it to his satisfaction. Therefore, punishment would ensue, normally pushups or other strenuous physical activity until the recruit was utterly exhausted, and then required to do more. This random scrambling of us recruits to the duty station and the demanding chores given by the duty officers continued for two or three hours, and then stopped so we recruits, not to mention the duty officers, could get some undisturbed sleep during what remained of the night. The next day we finished in-processing, which consisted of a medical exam, dental exam, vaccinations, first haircut, and clothing issue as illustrated in pictures 4, 5, 6, 7, 8, 9, and 10 at the end of the chapter.

To call what we got a haircut is a misnomer; it was a shearing. My full head of curly blond hair ended up on the floor with everyone else's hair, and we all had some laughs at how we looked bald. Little did we know that, for some of us, it was a glimpse into what the future had in store for us.

Everything was geared toward speed. Get with it, get it done, and get on to the next thing on the schedule. The Marines issuing clothing didn't ask your size or take measurements, except in the case of the dress uniforms, the greens and the tans. The reason they took measurements for those was probably the tradition that Marines look extra sharp in dress uniform, a cut above the other services. But as far as utility uniforms, underwear, etc., the Marines issuing clothing simply looked at you, guessed your size, and issued accordingly. It cut down on the time required, and as I said, everything was geared toward speed. If you were a size 36 and ended up with size 40 underwear and utilities, you made do with them; in other words, accommodate and innovate, two qualities Marines are famous for.

As far as the fancy dress blue uniform was concerned, the uniform that most agree is more than just a cut above those of the other services, we didn't get that uniform until the end of boot camp. I suppose the reason was that we had to earn the right to wear that uniform, and successfully completing boot camp was our rite of passage to earning that right.

It was at this time that we met our Senior Drill Instructor and that our small group from Omaha was combined with a number of other small groups having arrived from various locations in the Midwest and western part of the country, and officially designated as Platoon 245, 2nd Battalion, Marine Corps Recruit Training Command. After losing some recruits during boot camp for various reasons, primarily physical, our Platoon 245 numbered 80 souls at graduation three months later.

Our Senior Drill Instructor, SSgt. Beeson, whom I will refer to as SDI Beeson, would march us to the recruit training area of the base, which was on the south side of the base adjacent to the parade ground. The in-processing area, which we were leaving, was on the north side of the base in the attractive area of the Spanish architecture, palm lined streets and sidewalks I mentioned earlier. We recruits were about to experience a drastic change of scenery. The recruit training area, which would be our home for the next twelve weeks, did not have modern dormitory facilities like today. Living quarters consisted of numerous World War II quonset huts with concrete floors. As I remember, each quonset hut held twenty or more double bunks, and our platoon was quartered in two of them, with a third quonset hut as the duty hut for our two drill instructors' office and sleeping quarters. The World War II type quonset huts in which we lived are shown in picture 11, and the dormitory type recruit barracks that were built later on are shown in picture 12.

I remember SDI Beeson marching us down one of those attractive streets on the north side on the way to the south side recruit training area when we came abreast a BAM, a young lady Marine, and a quite attractive one. The drill instructors, as we found out later, referred to lady Marines as BAMs, the initials standing for broad-assed Marines. SDI Beeson marched us past the young lady, then called us to a halt and gave us "right face," which had us facing the lady. Then, as she passed, he said, "Alright maggots, take a good, long look. It's the last time you'll see a sight like that for the next twelve weeks." The lady Marine, aware of what our drill instructor was doing, tried to appear as provocative as possible while still maintaining proper decorum as a Marine. She succeeded.

Upon arrival in the recruit area, the Platoon was divided between two quonset huts. Each recruit was assigned a bunk, a footlocker for underwear, socks, toiletries, etc., and a wall locker for utility uniforms, dress uniforms, towels, boots, shoes, etc. Everything was to be regimented down to the last smallest detail. You've heard the saying, "There's a right way and a wrong way of doing things." In the Marine Corps, there is only one way of doing things, and that's the Marine way. Items in the footlocker were to be folded in a precise manner to a specific measurement and displayed in proper sequence. Items in the wall locker were to be hung in proper sequence. More on this later. The bed was made with sheets and blanket corners shaped with military precision shown in picture 13 and the covering pulled taunt enough so you could bounce a coin on it. And as shown in picture 14, the fold of the bed cover was to be precisely one bayonet length from the front of the mattress.

Obviously, no recruit was going to get all this perfect on the first try, or the second try, or even the third try. And from the moment we entered boot camp, it was drilled into us that perfection was the standard in everything we did. Perfection was the normal in the Maine Corps and nothing else was acceptable, which meant that every recruit experienced at least once, and usually more than once, having the drill instructor rip his bunk apart, throwing blankets, sheets, pillow and mattress onto the concrete floor for some minor offense, while loudly, in colorful, insulting, profane language commenting on the recruit's mental and cognitive capacities. Since I had preferred a top bunk, putting it all back together after my mattress and bedding ended up on the concrete floor was more difficult.

In-processing was finished, and we were settled in what would be our home for the next twelve weeks.

*"Freedom is not free,
but the U.S. Marine Corps
will pay most of your share."*

Ned Dolan, Marine and CIA officer

LEATHERNECK

1

2

3

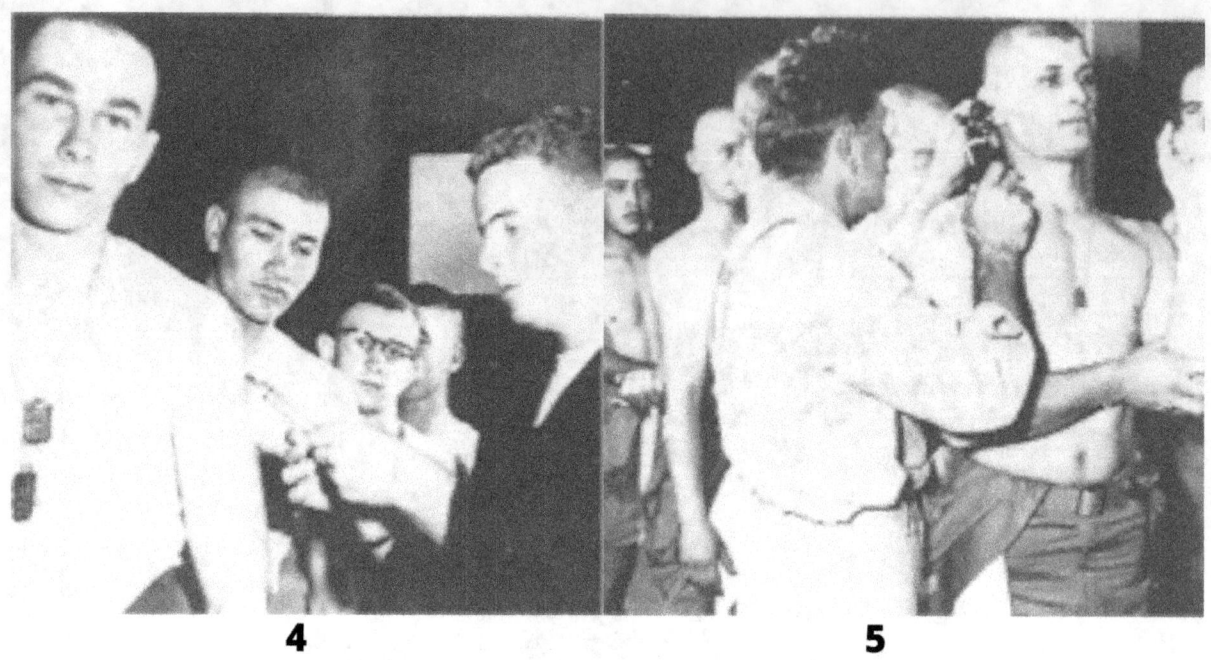

4

5

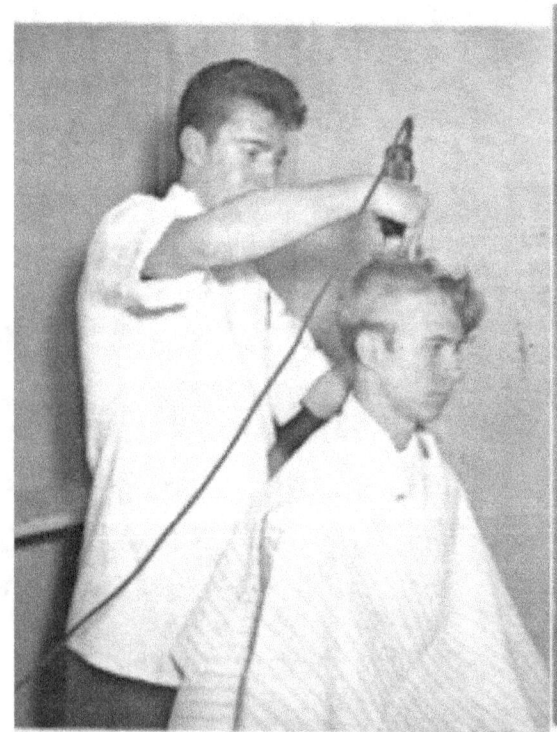

6

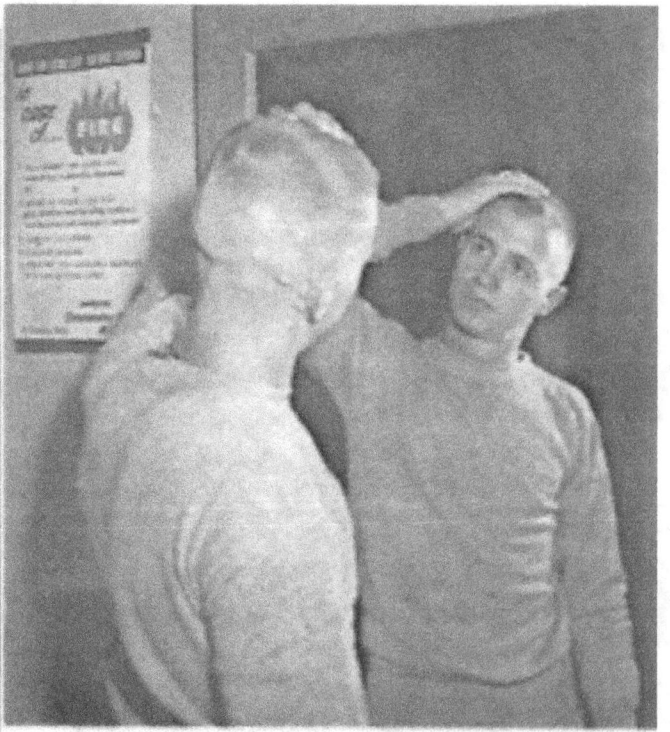

7

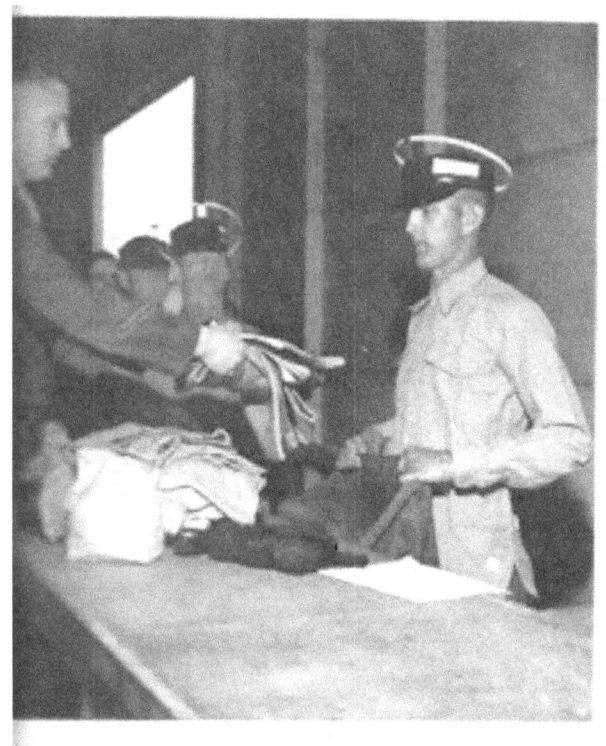

8

9

10

11

12

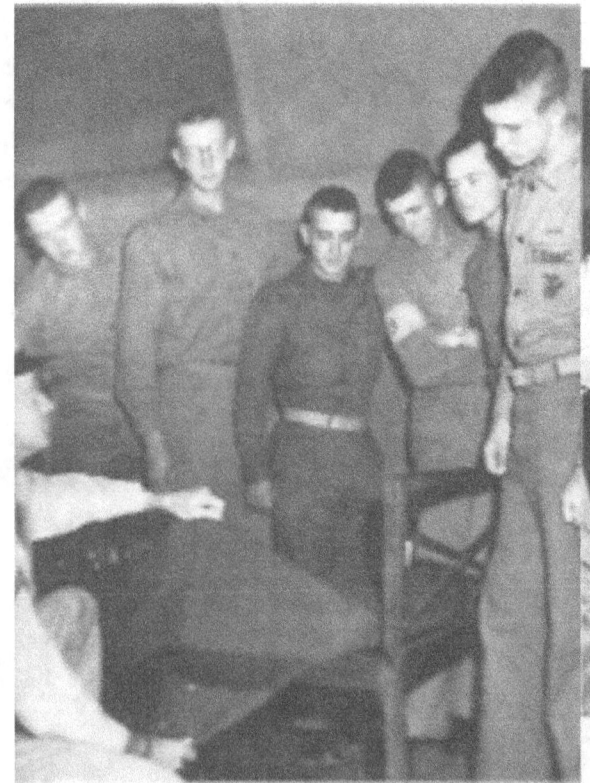
13

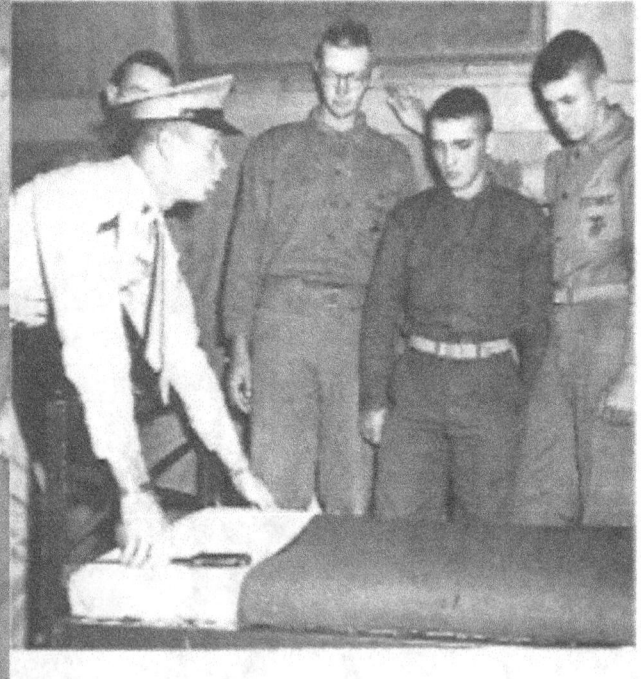
14

Chapter 3
The Drill Instructors

Let me introduce our drill instructors. Their pictures are shown at the end of the chapter. The Senior Drill Instructor, as mentioned, was SSgt. Beeson. You'll notice that I did not list his first name. I didn't know it. In fact, I'm sure none of us knew his first name all the way through boot camp. In our Platoon yearbook, presented to us upon graduation, his picture is obviously in it, but only with first and middle initial and last name. To this day, I don't know his first name, nor that of the Junior Drill Instructor.

Nor did we know whether they were married or bachelors. SDI Beeson had an impressive background, which by the way, we did not learn from him, but from being told by the JDI and other instructors we had in boot camp who knew him. When World War II broke out with the Japanese attack on Pearl Harbor, SDI Beeson was either in China or the Philippines, I forget which. At any rate, early in the war, he was captured by the Japanese and spent the remainder of it (nearly four years) in Japanese prison camps, with all the misery, suffering, torture that entailed. He endured and suffered it honorably, survived, and returned home after the war.

Five years later, during the Korean War, in the winter of Nov.-Dec. 1950, SDI Beeson was at the Chosin Reservoir in North Korea, one of the most brutal and bloody battles of the war, with heavy casualties and extreme physical and mental suffering. The Chosin Reservoir is listed with the most epic battles in Marine Corps history. The 1st Marine Division, with elements of the U.S. Army 7th Infantry Division, had crossed the 38th Parallel which divided North and South Korea, and advanced well into North Korea as far as the Chosin Reservoir. It was at this time the Chinese Army entered the war to assist the North Koreans in their objective of defeating the United Nation's forces led by the United States and take over South Korea.

The 1st Marine Division was surrounded and vastly outnumbered by an estimated 120,000 Chinese Communist infantry and was on the verge of annihilation. Temperatures plummeted to —36 degrees F. In the bitter cold, frostbite was common, weapons malfunctioned, and the Marines had to urinate on their rifles to keep the bolts from freezing shut. This, combined with the brutal terrain, and having to beat back wave after wave of Chinese mass attacks, resulted in the American forces barely holding on. The death toll soared.

The only route to survival was to break out to the sea along a treacherous, winding, snow-packed and icy road to a port 70 miles to the rear where allied ships could pick them up. This, of course, involved a retreat; however, the word "retreat" is not in the Marine Corps dictionary. Therefore, it was referred to as "an attack in a different direction." I believe it was either the Marine 1st Division commander, General Oliver P. Smith, or the overall Marine commander, General "Chesty" Puller, who made the comment, "The poor bastards have us surrounded. Now we can attack them in any direction."

And so, the withdrawal from the Chosin Reservoir, and the terrible fighting and suffering to reach that seaport 70 miles away was not a retreat; it came to be known as "an attack in a different direction." Nearly 6000 Americans were dead or missing, and thousands more wounded. But the Chinese Communists paid a much higher price - an estimated 50,000 casualties. The Marines made a deep impression on the Chinese during this initial battle. It is said that one of the Chinese commanders said to his comrades, "Don't mess with the Marine 1st Division if you can help it. They run to the fight." The Marines who fought and survived the horrific battles at Chosin Reservoir are referred to as the Chosin Few. Our SDI Beeson was one of those Chosin Few. If SDI Beeson were alive today, and walked into a room where I was sitting, I would snap to attention as a Lieutenant Colonel to show my deep admiration and respect for his extraordinary service as a United States Marine.

I don't remember the name of our first Junior Drill Instructor because he didn't last long before SDI Beeson fired him. The circumstances were as follows. After two weeks of boot camp, and one night when the Junior DI had the duty, there was a movie playing in the base theater that he wanted to see. And so, he took our platoon to see the movie. Now, going to the movie was one of the supreme pleasures and highest rewards the recruits could experience in boot camp, which should give the reader an impression of just how restrictive Marine boot camp really was.

Those two or three hours at the movie allowed the recruits to escape the quonset hut and parade ground area and enjoy an environment with human beings other than recruits, both male and female. And we were even allowed to have popcorn, soda, candy, etc. Of course, the recruits were kept together, and not allowed to mingle with the crowd. We were marched to a section where we could get popcorn, etc., and then taken to an area reserved for recruit seating. No one was allowed to leave their seat during the movie. If nature called, that was tough; you just held it. Nevertheless, going to the movie was a special, special treat which the drill instructors used very, very sparingly to reward their recruits for excellent performance and accomplishment. During our three months in boot camp, we were taken to a movie only twice after this.

For our JDI to take us to the movie after only two weeks in boot camp was unheard of, and apparently considered a major infraction of protocol by SDI Beeson. The JDI was gone the next day, not to be seen or heard of again. He was replaced by our new Junior Drill Instructor, Sgt. S.A. Chapman.

JDI Chapman was a big, burly, imposing and somewhat frightening giant of a man who remained our JDI until graduation. Whereas SDI Beeson was hard, tough, but fair as far as Marine standards go, JDI Chapman seemed to have more of a sadistic streak in him. He relished calling reveille at 5:00 a.m. turning on the lights, and then proceed to dump the bunks, including occupants, of those he considered late in responding, on the concrete floor. Our fear of SDI Beeson was tinged with admiration and respect. Our fear of JDI Chapman was just that - fear.

These two career Marines, SDI Beeson and JDI Chapman would control every aspect of our lives for that long, long, twelve weeks, that three months, that eighty-five days, that two thousand forty hours of being transformed from civilian to maggot to United States Marine.

Our next experience was to be indoctrinated into some rules of engagement that would dictate our behavior during those twelve weeks. These rules were laid down by the drill instructors, were set in stone, and woe to the unfortunate recruit who violated any of them.

**Senior Drill Instructor
S/Sgt. Beeson**

**Junior Drill Instructor
Sgt. Chapman**

"Retreat hell! We've just got here!"

Marine Officer
Belleau Wood
June 1918

Chapter 4
Rules for Recruits

The rules governing the recruit's daily life were simple, straightforward, and uncompromising as follows:

1. When the Drill Instructor entered the barracks at 5:00 a.m., turned on the lights and bellowed "reveille," the recruits had fifteen to twenty minutes to make up their bunks, go to the "head," (which is Navy/Marine language for bathroom), and shave, shower, get back to their bunk, get dressed and be ready to fall out in formation outside. If you were late, punishment would follow, probably in the form of pushups or other strenuous physical activity.

2. A recruit was never to speak to a Drill Instructor without asking permission. His request was to be prefaced with and ended with "Sir," as follows: "SIR, Private Ahrens requests permission to speak to the Drill Instructor. SIR!" The Drill Instructor's inevitable reply would be, "I can't hear you, maggot!" Whereupon the recruit would repeat the request louder. This would go for a few repetitions until the recruit was yelling at the top of his voice and the Drill Instructor would finally say, "Speak!" Again, every statement spoken to a Drill Instructor was to be prefaced and ended with, "SIR!"

3. A recruit was never to pass in front of a Drill Instructor marching his platoon. He was to wait until they had passed or were called to a halt. I will discuss my harsh punishment for violating this rule in a later chapter.

4. A recruit was never to sit or lay on his bunk during the day. If he had to sit while cleaning his rifle or shining his boots, for example, he would sit on his footlocker. I'll have more to say on violating this rule later on.

5. While eating in the mess hall, the recruit was not to slouch or lean over his meal, but to eat it in a precise and disciplined manner at near attention.

6. A recruit was never to give an excuse for having failed to accomplish a task or obeying a command. When asked why he failed, his reply was to be, "No excuse, Sir!" Let me give a hypothetical example of this for emphasis. Assume you are instructed to be at a certain place at a certain time, but on the way you are struck by lightning and knocked unconscious. You wake up and proceed to your meeting, but you are late. You have a valid reason for being late, but when asked why you are late, your reply is to be simply, "No excuse, Sir!" Now to a civilian or someone unfamiliar with the military, this may appear silly. But let's consider it for a moment. During military combat operations, failure to obey a command, or be in the right place at the right time, can result in defeat, disaster, and death for yourself and others. Mission accomplishment, obedience to orders, and doing whatever is necessary to accomplish the assigned task is drilled into the recruit from the moment he/she enters boot camp and throughout their time in the military until it is a quality of character instilled in them. And that quality of character can be described

as, "Failure is not an option!" Perhaps this is one of the many reasons that industries and businesses have a preference for hiring veterans.

7. A recruit was never to smoke unless the Drill Instructor announced that "the smoking lamp is lit." "The smoking lamp is lit" or "the smoking lamp is out" are terms used by the Navy aboard ship to regulate smoking because of the increased potential for fire and explosion due to fuel and ammunition. Smoking lamp was a figurative term and the Marines adopted it. Punishment for violating this rule was harsh, which I will describe later.

8. The only time the recruit was to walk was during marching. Any other time the recruit was moving from one point to another it would be at "double time," that is, running.

Speaking of marching, the activity the recruit would spend the most time on during boot camp would be drill formation. As mentioned, Marines are always striving for perfection, and this is only achieved after many, many, hours and days of instruction and practice in drill, drill, and more drill. Drill formation was a daily part of the recruit's life in boot camp, and a frequent part of his life after boot camp throughout his career. I think this is evidenced when people view members of the various services marching in parades, ceremonies, and other occasions. The Marines usually stand out. Drill formation develops discipline, precision, teamwork, unity, and esprit de corps, the mark of a Marine.

The Drill Instructors set the rules for every aspect of the recruit's life and dictated the time the recruit was given to accomplish each task, whether it be eating a meal, cleaning one's rifle, shining one's boots, doing the laundry, right up to the time allotted for sleep. Speaking of doing the laundry, there were no washing machines or dryers. We did it the old fashioned way - by hand as shown in pictures 1, 2, and 3 at the end of the chapter. Also, we were introduced to, and gained proficiency in, the art of sewing. When a button needed sewing on, or a tear needed mending, the recruit was his own seamstress, as depicted on the picture page as Illustration 4. A sewing kit was included in our original supply Issue.

Time was set aside for recruits to write letters home. Woe be to the recruit whose parents had contacted base authorities complaining that they had not heard from their son since he left for boot camp. Mail call was a highlight of our thoroughly regimented life. The Drill Instructors controlled every waking moment of our lives, but they had to allow us time to read mail and write home. This was our connection to the outside world, and we savored it. As I recall, mail call was once a week. Pictures 5 and 6, at the end of the chapter, show a typical mail call and a couple recruits devouring their mail. We saved all our letters from home and our loved ones and reread them during rare moments of leisure, especially the married recruits.

Recruits were allowed to have visitors at the visitor's center on the other side of the base. The time was limited to one or two hours and the recruit could only have three visitors during the three months at boot camp. Drill instructors hated this because it meant the recruit was free of their control and discipline for that time. The recruit was free to smoke as many cigarettes and eat as much pogey bait (the term for candy bars and other sweets) as he wanted. The limit of only three visitors during the three months applied to the married recruits also. The Drill Instructors' comment to the married recruits was, "If the Marine Corps wanted you to have a wife, they would have issued you one." I'm not sure whether SDI Beeson and JDI Chapman were married or not. They never mentioned their marital status and, of course, none of us would dare pose the question to them. But thinking back on it, I'm almost certain they were both bachelor career Marines. I had one visitor during those three months. My cousin Ross, who was in the Marines stationed at Barstow Marine Corps Base, Calif., during a weekend of liberty, came to see me. Having been through it, he knew what that free time with a visitor meant to a recruit, and I really appreciated his providing it to me.

SDI Beeson had appointed one of our members as Right Guide of the Platoon. The Right Guide served as the coordinator, the intermediate authority between the Drill Instructors and the rest of the recruits. The title "Right Guide" referred to the individual's position at the head of the marching formation, responsible for leading the formation in correct response to the Drill Instructor's commands. The Right Guide was in charge and responsible for the recruits' activities and behavior when the Drill Instructors were not physically present. The Drill Instructors would pass instructions to the recruits through the Right Guide, who was then responsible to see that those instructions were complied with. This meant that any violation of those instructions would result in punishment not only to the offender or offenders, but also to the Right Guide for failing in his leadership responsibility.

After one week of boot camp, while marching in drill formation, SDI Beeson called the formation to a halt, told his original choice as Right Guide that he was fired and to get back into rank formation. He then called me out of formation to the front position and informed me that I was Right Guide. Why me? I had no idea. Perhaps he didn't like the other guy's marching and liked mine. Who knows? At any rate, SDI Beeson told me that if I xx#z!x# up, he would fire me too. Well, I didn't get fired. I held the position for the remaining 11 weeks of boot camp, and I learned some important lessons of leadership and its demands, hard decisions, loneliness, and yes, satisfactions. The result was that upon graduation, I was one of only two of our platoon of recruits that were promoted to Private First Class right out of boot camp, which made my fellow graduate and I eligible for sea school which was a big deal. I'll say more about that toward the end of the book. And so, that skinny kid who the folks back home thought could never be a Marine became Right Guide of the platoon and one of two distinguished graduates, marching at the head of the platoon shown in picture 7.

During this time frame (1950s), it was common practice for judges to give young criminals, usually notorious gang members, a choice. Either go to jail, or go into the Marine Corps. I know that many liberals today wouldn't believe our courts would allow this, but it is true. As I said, it usually involved violent gang members from gang centers like "Hell's Kitchen" and others in the major cities. The Marine Drill Instructors loved to get these guys in boot camp. We had two or three of them in our platoon. As I previously mentioned, the Drill Instructor's mode of operation was to break down the recruits completely, rid them of their civilian identity, and then rebuild them into Marines with all the character traits involved in that identity. How did those tough, hardened, gang members respond to that treatment? Well, after a week or so of the harsh, physical and mental pressure suffered under the Drill Instructors, those tough, hardened, former gang members were sobbing and scared shitless just like the rest of us.

But, as that long, long twelve weeks of boot camp continued, a gradual change of attitude and demeanor came upon those former gang members. Like the rest of us, they strove to excel in the training courses, and with the rest of us, were being welded into a unit, not a gang unit, but into a military unit of precision and discipline. And after those twelve weeks of boot camp, those former gang members, with the rest of us in full dress uniform, marched in our graduation parade and were damn proud to bear the title of United States Marine. Those judges who gave those gang members the choice of jail or the Marine Corps knew what they were doing. And those Marine Drill Instructors did more to turn those gang members into productive citizens than a roomful of social workers could have done.

1

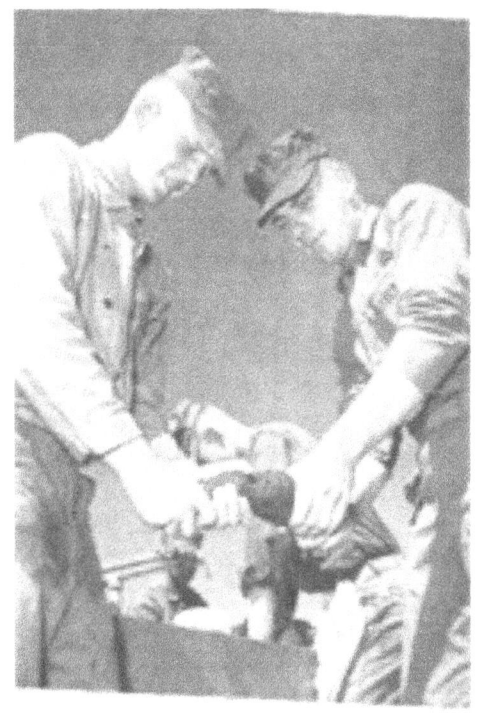

2

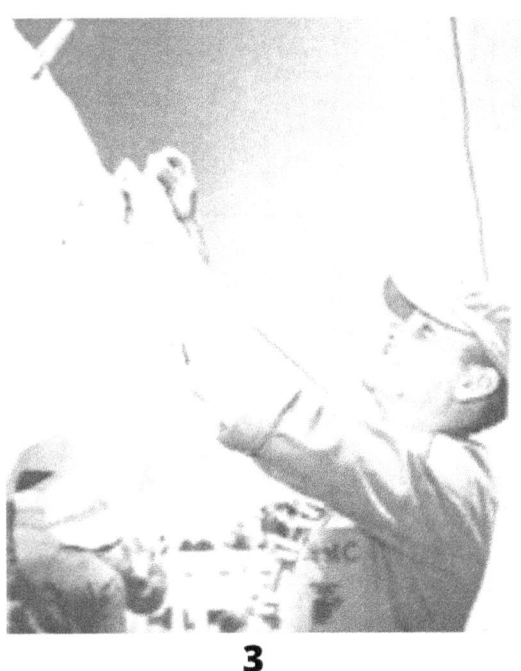

3

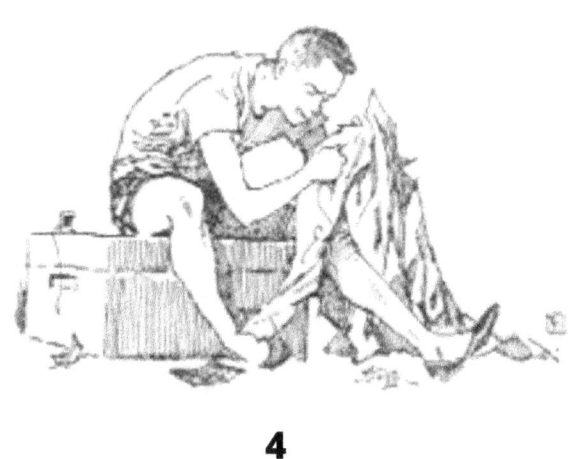

4

5

6

7

Chapter 5
The Marine's Companion

Early on in boot camp, the Marine recruit is introduced to what would be his constant companion for the remainder of his time in the Corps - his rifle. For our time period, it was the 9 1/2 pound, 30 caliber, semi-automatic M-1 rifle, the standard combat rifle in World War II, Korea, and for some time afterward.

First, it is necessary to understand the relationship between a Marine and his rifle. Every Marine is designated first and foremost as a rifleman. It makes no difference what your specialty is, whether infantryman, artilleryman, pilot, explosive disposal specialist, lawyer, cook, administrator, doctor, tanker, or what have you. You are first and foremost a rifleman, trained as such, and can be called at any time to take your rifle and fill a position in the line of battle. Therefore, it is required that you maintain rifle qualification year after year. Marines take pride in the fact that they are first and foremost rifleman, and their history and tradition is filled with examples of Marines with various specialties filling in as combat infantrymen with great courage and honor. The relationship between a Marine and his rifle is best described by the Creed of the United States Marine entitled "My Rifle," which goes as follows:

My Rifle

"This is my rifle. There are many like it, but this one is mine. My rifle is my best friend. I must master it as I must master my life. My rifle without me is useless. Without my rifle I am useless. I must fire my rifle true. I must shoot straighter than my enemy who is trying to kill me. I must shoot him before he shoots me. I will…My rifle and myself know that what counts in war is not the rounds we fire, the noise of our burst, nor the smoke we make. We know that it is the hits that count. We will hit. I will learn my rifle as a brother. I will learn its weaknesses, its strengths, its parts, its accessories, its sights, and its barrel. I will ever guard it against the ravages of weather and damage. I will keep my rifle clean and ready, even as I am clean and ready. We will become part of each other. We will. My rifle and myself are the defenders of my country. We are the masters of our enemy. So be it until there is no enemy, but peace!"

This may sound a bit over the top, but then Marines tend to take things to the extreme. We recruits would become totally familiar with our rifle, its every part, its every mode of operation. We would be able to disassemble it and reassemble it in a matter of seconds blindfolded. Sixty-seven years later, I can tell you my rifle's serial number - 1572688. The most important phase of training in Marine boot camp was rifle qualification, a three-week program conducted at Camp Matthews, a Marine rifle range located approximately 30 miles north from the Recruit Depot. I will cover this in a later chapter.

Along with our rifles, we were given strict warning to never, never, refer to our rifle as a gun. To help us remember that we were given a rhyme to memorize. If a recruit forgot and violated this rule, he would end up marching at the rear of the platoon for as long as the Drill Instructor decided, while yelling this rhyme:

"This is my rifle" (pointing to his rifle),
    "this is my gun" (pointing to his crotch),
"This is for killing" (pointing to his rifle),
    "this is for fun." (pointing to his crotch).

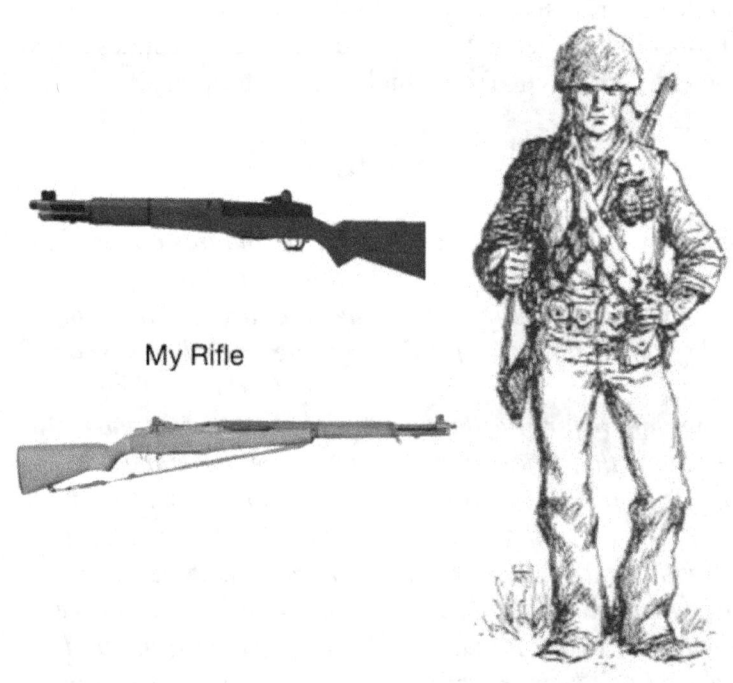

My Rifle

Chapter 6
To the Last Man

I'm not sure what caused it. We were all still asleep and hadn't done anything yet to warrant punishment. Perhaps the JDI had a bad night and wanted to take it out on someone. And who better to take it out on than his bunch of Marine recruits who he had total control over. At any rate, he turned on the lights at 5:00 a.m., shouted reveille, and ordered us to get dressed and fall out in formation with our M-1 rifles.

He marched us to the "grinder," which is what we called that 2 mile circumference parade ground. Once there, he called us to a halt, gave us "port arms," which was to hold that 9 1/2 pound M-1 rifle out in front with arms rigid, and then he ordered "double time", and we started the run. We assumed that after we ran for awhile he would call it off and we would return to the barracks area. But then, as the run continued and continued, it became clear to us that this was a run until the last man dropped when the JDI began taunting us saying, "You all are hoping I'll drop dead from a heart attack but let me tell you something: I'll be on my feet when you all are on your hands and knees gasping and puking your guts out."

You can imagine how heavy that 9 1/2 pound M-1 rifle became, holding it at arm's length, as we ran. We would bring it in closer to our body to relieve the tension, and the JDI would curse at us to get it back out to where it belonged. As the run progressed, and with the realization that it wasn't going to stop until we all dropped, an overriding determination seemed to take over in us - a determination to outlast the JDI, to be still running when he reached the end of his endurance. After all, he was in his mid to late 30s, and we were all in our teens and very early twenties. Surely some of us, a few of us, could outlast him.

As exhaustion started to have its effects, I developed a way to keep going. I would look ahead and pick a landmark - a building, a tree, a sign, or some other object adjacent to the parade ground - and tell myself that I could go at least that much farther, and then I could drop out. As I approached that landmark, I would pick another one some distance ahead, and convince myself that I could go that far and then drop out. This worked for awhile, but it wasn't long before nothing could induce me to go farther. The breathing was labored, I was feeling nauseous, and even before the run started, I was feeling some of the symptoms of flu, probably because of the cold, wet, weather. I finally fell to my knees gasping.

Most of the platoon made it past the one mile point; some even made it to the 2 mile point, and a few past that. I believe I made it just over a mile and a half. With my coughing, wheezing, the JDI, who was aware of my flu symptoms, asked me if I wanted to go to sick bay, the first-aid station. I answered, "No! Absolutely not!" I knew that if I went to sick bay, and they kept me there for two days or more, I would probably be dropped back to another platoon. There was no way I was going to chance that.

Of course, all the recruits eventually dropped out, on their hands and knees some sobbing, all gasping, and some puking, with the JDI berating us and calling us a bunch of xy&q*<# pansies, and worse, which I won't mention. And yes, he was still on his feet when the rest of us were not. As I said, perhaps something had put him into a rage, and we were the handy objects upon which he could vent that rage. Thinking about it later, I realized that the determination that I and undoubtedly others had to outlast the JDI stemmed from our anger towards him for his treatment of us, and that motivated us and gave us that extra energy to push ourselves beyond the point where we would normally give up. And I'm sure that it was exactly that attitude the JDI was hoping would result from his treatment, taunts, and insults.

Stirring up our anger and resentment against them to motivate us to go beyond our normal limits of endurance was a tactic the drill instructors used throughout boot camp, and beyond a doubt, it was effective.

Chapter 7
No Favoritism

I mentioned how I was selected as Right Guide of the Platoon by SDI Beeson, and how, with the intermediate authority and responsibility delegated to me by the Drill Instructors with that position, I learned a great deal about leadership and its demands and tough decisions. Let me give you an example.

I previously referred to one of my fellow recruits, John E., a high school classmate of mine and neighbor, who I was surprised to see in our group of seven leaving from Omaha. One afternoon, while we were sitting on our footlockers cleaning our rifles, I noticed John laying on his bunk, a violation of one of the aforementioned rules. As Right Guide of the platoon, the Drill Instructors expected me to prevent such violation when they were not present. I told John to get off his bunk, and that he knew the rule as well as the rest of us. It was obvious that John was sick with flu-like symptoms. He asked me, "Please Darrell, don't make me get up; I feel terrible, please let me lay here!" I felt sorry for him, and so I let him lay on his bunk. But I took precautions. The front door of the quonset hut was open, and the passageway leading to the quonset hut which contained the Drill Instructors' office, was in clear view. I positioned a couple guys near that door and told them to keep a sharp lookout, and if they saw a Drill Instructor coming our way, to pass the word so I could get John off his bunk.

I thought our violation of the bunk rule was safe from being discovered, but I had not anticipated one thing. The Drill Instructor did make his rounds, but he came in the back door of the quonset hut instead of the front door. The recruits near the back door called us to attention, but it was too late. The Drill Instructor had progressed far enough to where he saw John laying on his bunk. He didn't say anything and simply walked through the barracks, out the front door, and back to his office in the duty hut. But I knew what was coming.

And sure enough! The call soon came in a loud, bellowing voice, "Right Guide to the duty hut!" I received a royal chewing out with profane references to my character, leadership failure, violation of the Drill Instructors' trust, etc., etc. Also, the Drill Instructors put me through about thirty minutes of physical endurance testing - pushups, setups, running in place, etc., until I was totally exhausted. One of the endurance tests was for me to assume the duckwalk position, with my back to the wall and my rear end elevated. The strain on the legs and the back eventually became extreme, and the relief was to let the back slide down the wall until the rear end reached the floor and you could assume the sitting position. To convince me not to seek such relief, one of the Drill Instructors held a bayonet underneath me, with the sharp end pointed at my elevated rear end. After about thirty minutes of all this, I was an exhausted mess. The Drill Instructors told me to get my ass back to the barracks and perform the duties they had given me as Right Guide of the Platoon.

For some reason, SDI Beeson didn't fire me as Right Guide as he had done to my predecessor. I don't know why. Perhaps he saw something in me that I didn't see in myself. At any rate, I never again willfully violated any of the Drill Instructors' rules, and I remained faithful to the intermediate authority and responsibility they had given me as their representative to the other recruits when they were not present. And I never again played favoritism, and I treated all my fellow recruits equally. I went back to the barracks, told my friend John E. to get his ass off his bunk, and if he was going to die, he would die on the concrete floor and not on his bunk.

Two other observations regarding this event. First, John was never punished by the Drill Instructors for his breaking the bunk rule. I, the Right Guide, was the only one punished. And this points to one of the cardinal rules of the military, and especially the Marine Corps. The leader is always responsible for the performance of those under his/her command. It was one of the many leadership lessons I would learn as a young 19 year old Marine recruit and Right Guide, and a lesson that served me well later on as an Air Force officer and fighter pilot.

Second, my decision to no longer play favoritism, treat everyone equally, and insist on compliance with the rules even when the Drill Instructors weren't around, caused some anger and resentment with some of my fellow recruits. Remember those former gang members I mentioned? One of them came to me and said, "Ahrens, we have to put up with you during boot camp, but when that's over, your days are numbered. You're a dead man!" I shook it off, and responded with something to the effect, "Yeah, yeah, whatever." But as I previously mentioned, as boot camp progressed, those former gang members underwent an attitude change and responded to the challenge, thanks to the Drill Instructors' arts of persuasion, and by graduation were proud Marines. That threat to me was never mentioned again, and obviously nothing came of it, since I'm still alive.

Again, the leadership lesson: As a leader, it's nice, but it's not important that you be liked; however, it's vitally important that you be respected!

Chapter 8
Tragedy at Parris Island

After we had been in boot camp for little over a month, we were informed of a tragedy that had occurred at our sister Marine Recruit Depot at Parris Island, South Carolina. On April 8, 1956, a Junior Drill Instructor led his recruits on a night exercise in a swampy tidal creek on Parris Island near the base. The JDI marched the platoon along the creek bed, but many strayed into deep water, resulting in the drowning deaths of six recruits.

The tragedy gained national and international media coverage. The JDI was court-marshaled amidst an outcry of public condemnation over the "brutality" of Marine Corps training. However, many came to the JDI's defense, pointing out such harsh training was necessary to survive in combat, and that night maneuvers and marching were very common. The Marine Corps Commandant, General Randolph Pate, testified at the JDI's trial. But the most famous witness to testify was General Lewis "Chesty" Puller, the most decorated Marine in the history of the Corps. General Puller called the incident "a deplorable accident," but one that did not warrant court-marshal. He said that discipline was the most important factor in military training, and quoted Napoleon as saying that an army becomes a "mob" without it. General Puller also mentioned his experiences during the Korean War, and that one of the shortfalls in training was the lack of night training.

The JDI was acquitted of manslaughter, as well as acquitted of all intentional or willful misconduct toward the men under his command. He was, however, found guilty of negligent homicide. He was sentenced to three months in the brig and reduction to the rank of Private, and was allowed to remain in the Corps.

When our Drill Instructors informed us of the tragedy, they said that we were probably thinking that they would ease up a bit on the toughness and harshness of our training because of it. And they were right; we were thinking and hoping that. They told us to forget that, that things were only going to get tougher. And they made good on that promise.

It is interesting that, a year later in 1957, the Marine Corps provided assistance to Hollywood in the making of the movie "The D.I.," which Jack Webb both directed and starred in as the title character, the tough Drill Instructor. The movie depicted a patriotic, pro-Marine Corps point of view on the need for high-pressure, tough standards in basic training, and the duty and responsibility of the Drill Instructor to provide that training. The movie was very popular with the public. The movie's poster is shown on the next page.

Chapter 9
The Smoking Lamp

I mentioned "The Smoking Lamp" previously, the shipboard origin of the term, and its use to permit smoking or forbid smoking. For the Drill Instructors to call a break in whatever we were doing and say, "the smoking lamp is lit," meant that the platoon was performing well and the D.I. was pleased. The smokers in the platoon anxiously awaited those words. However, in this case as in all cases, the Drill Instructors were not generous with complements, praise, or rewards. By far, the normal case as far as smoking was concerned, was "The Smoking Lamp is out." Therefore, there was always the temptation for the smokers to sneak a smoke when the Drill Instructors weren't around. The favorite time to do this was at night when everyone was in bed asleep, including the Drill Instructors. The offender would go outside, hug the barracks wall to stay out of sight of the Marine guard, enjoy a quick smoke, and return to bed. Of course, the Drill Instructors also knew this routine. There was no trick the recruits could think of that the Drill Instructors had not experienced before and kept a watchful eye for.

And so, it was one morning around 2:00 a.m. while we were sound asleep, that the barracks lights came on and SDI Beeson yelling at us to get out of bed and fall in outside at attention. It was dark, it was raining, and the combination of the rain and the sea breeze coming from the ocean, and our being only in our skivvies, made it miserably cold. SDI Beeson informed us of the reason for this rude interruption of our sleep. One of our number had been caught outside the barracks sneaking a cigarette. The offender was standing next to SDI Beeson in front of the formation standing at attention. With the outside lighting, we could see that in his hand he had a pack of Pall Mall cigarettes, the long, unfiltered kind.

Since the offender's craving for a cigarette was so strong that he felt compelled to violate one of the cardinal rules, SDI Beeson was going to ensure that his craving was satisfied. Upon the D.I.s instruction, the recruit took a cigarette out of the pack, put it in his mouth, slowly chewed it up, and then swallowed it. He then took another cigarette out of the pack, slowly chewed it up, and then swallowed it. Then another, and another. He kept this up until he had consumed about half the pack, at which time he became ill and started vomiting. SDI Beeson called it off, dismissed us all back to our bunks soaking wet and shivering cold, and left the offending recruit to clean up his mess before returning to his bunk. The experience served to make the smokers a lot more hesitant to try and sneak a smoke when the smoking lamp was not lit. That included myself, of course, but I had another strong reason for not attempting to sneak a smoke. That was the fact that I was Right Guide of the Platoon, and honor bound not to violate the trust that the Drill Instructors had placed in me.

One other important lesson to be learned from this event, and which would be relearned time and time again during boot camp, was that when one member of the unit disobeyed an order or instruction, not only he, but all members of the unit. would suffer the consequences. Why is this? Because in combat, if one member of the unit fails to perform his duty, or chooses to ignore an order or instruction, the result can be mission failure and/or the death of other members of the unit. Unit cohesion is the foundation of the term "band of brothers." A Marine will, as I'm sure members of the other services will, go to the extremes of life and death to avoid letting down or failing his brothers. However, concerning the recruit whose punishment we had to witness while cold, wet, and miserable, he was not too popular with the rest of us for a time.

> *"You cannot exaggerate about the Marines. They are convinced to the point of arrogance that they are the most ferocious fighters on earth. And the amusing thing about it is that they are."*
>
> *Father Kevin Keaney*
> *1st Marine Division Chaplain*
> *Korean War*

Chapter 10
Initial Training

The twelve weeks of boot camp were basically divided into three stages - five weeks of initial training at the main base in San Diego, three weeks at the rifle range at Camp Matthews, north of San Diego, and four weeks of final training back in San Diego.

A major part of the initial training phase, as I previously noted, was drill formation instruction. Even when we marched to the mess hall for meals, before we entered the building, the D.I. would give us facing movements, have us march in place, and perform other drill movements. As Right Guide, I marched in front of the Platoon, as shown in a previous photograph, and as the title implies, the formation would guide on me. If I messed up, the entire formation would be out of step or sequence, and I would be the subject of some very salty language by the D.I. Precision, perfection, was the goal, and as time went on and the unending hours of drill progressed, so our precision and sharpness increased, but it was never good enough for SDI Beeson and JDI Chapman. Recruits who constantly were out of step, out of sequence, were sometimes forced to march at a distance to the rear of the formation, while in a loud voice referring to themselves in a profane, insulting manner, dictated by the Drill Instructors. The harsh, humiliating, treatment of us recruits by the Drill Instructors was not designed as punishment, but as incentive for us to strive to improve and excel.

Along with the constant drill were the numerous formal inspections. I previously mentioned the inspection called "junk on the bunk," where all items in the footlocker - utility uniforms, footwear, hats, gloves, underwear, toiletries, etc., were laid out on the bunk, as shown in picture 1 at the end of the chapter. The picture shows the exact placement of each item to be laid out on the bunk, neatly, folded precisely, and in the designated order. I also mentioned that if one flaw was discovered by the DI, which virtually every recruit experienced at one time or another, it would result in all the items on the bunk, and the bunk itself with pillow, sheets, blanket, and mattress, strewn on the concrete floor.

Picture 2 shows the contents of the wall locker with dress uniforms, towels, overcoat, raincoat, etc., and their precise and orderly display. Here too, if the DI found a flaw in the display, the contents of the wall locker would be strewn about the recruit's bunk area. The wall locker shown in the picture is obviously not a recruit's wall locker since the uniforms have rank insignia on the sleeves. Nevertheless, the display and the designated order of the contents would be the same, whether a recruit's wall locker or a graduate Marines.

Picture 3 shows us with our M-1 rifles and combat marching packs on our backs. I am in the front of the photo as Right Guide, with my classmate and neighbor John E. to my left. This combat marching pack, shown in picture 4, contained certain items to be taken into combat such as rations, toilet articles, undershirt, drawers, socks, mess gear, and poncho, with bayonet and entrenching tool attached to it. When laid out on the parade ground for inspection, the helmet, cartridge belt, and rifle which would be carried on the person, were included with the other items, as shown in the picture. Picture 5 shows the marching packs spread out on the parade ground with the items neatly arranged on it in the designated order, and the DI inspecting them. Picture 6 shows the D.I., having discovered a mistake in the recruit's display, kicking the items away from him in disgust, leaving the recruit's carefully ordered display a random mess.

The most important inspection was the rifle inspection, conducted frequently. It could also be an impressive thing to watch. As the Drill Instructor went through the line, stopping in front of each recruit, the recruit would sharply, and I emphasis sharply, bring his rifle from order arms to port arms, as shown in the pictures 7, 8, and 9, and slam the cartridge chamber lever to the rear to open the chamber for inspection.

To give the reader an idea of the precision required in drill movements with the rifle, let me give the instructions for going from order arms to port arms contained in my 67-year-old personal copy of Guidebook for Marines:

```
ORDER ARMS TO PORT ARMS. COMMAND: 1. Port 2. ARMS. (ONE) At the command
ARMS, raise the rifle with the right hand and carry it diagonally across
the front of the body until the right hand is in front of and slightly
to the left of the face so that the barrel is up, butt in front of the
right hip, barrel bisecting the angle of the neck and the left shoulder.
At the same time, grasp the rifle at the balance with the left hand,
palm toward the body. (TWO) Carry the right hand to the small of the
stock, grasping it, palm down, holding the right forearm horizontal;
left elbow resting against the body; the plane of the rifle parallel
to and about four inches in front of the center of the body, barrel
extending upward and to the left at an angle of 45 degrees.
```

The D.I. would grab the rifle with his right hand, slapping the stock sharply with the palm of his hand. The recruit would immediately release the rifle and move his hands out of the way down to his side. If he was slow in doing this, he would incur the D. I.s, wrath. And then, the D.I. would inspect the recruit's rifle, and it was a thing of beauty to behold as the D.I. handled that 9 1/2 pound M-1 rifle like a cheerleader's baton. Each D.I. had their personal routine of inspection, some fancier than others. Twisting the rifle around, he would carefully inspect the stock for scratches and gouges as shown in picture 10. Twirling it, he would inspect the metal buttplate and all metal parts of the rifle for cleanliness and absence of any sign of rust. Flipping the rifle end over end and catching it with the barrel pointed down, he would peer down the barrel, as shown picture 11, to ensure that it was clean and free of any sign of rust.

When finished with the inspection, he would flip the rifle over and assume the port arms position to present the rifle back to the recruit. The recruit would then imitate the D.I.'s previous action in grabbing the rifle by slapping the palm of his hand against the stock, grab the rifle out of the D.I.s hands, assume the port arms position while closing the cartridge chamber, and then assume the order arms position. The steps for going from port arms to order arms are shown in pictures 12, 13, 14, and 15, along with the narrative describing the movements. All movements were to be sharp, aggressive, well-defined, and precise. Any slowness or lack of aggressiveness in accomplishing these movements would gain the recruit a profane insult from the D.I. and probably some strenuous physical exercise along with it.

The worst possible thing that could happen during rifle inspection was for the D.I. to discover rust on the weapon, or in the barrel. Even a speck of rust was a major infraction and dealt with as such. We heard stories of Marines being sent to the brig at Quantico for a time because they allowed rust to soil their rifle. Remember the creed of the United States Marine entitled "My Rifle," given in a previous chapter entitled "The Marine's Companion?" Well, to allow rust to invade one's rifle was tantamount to allowing a stranger to violate a close friend. Thus, an activity we spent a great deal of time on was making sure our rifles set a new standard for cleanliness as shown with the recruits in pictures 16, 17, and 18, with 16 being yours truly.

During one of our rifle inspections, one of our recruits was found to have a spot of rust on his rifle. With the policy that when one member commits a violation, all members share the consequences, we all suffered for it. Our Drill Instructors marched us to an area that had lots of sand. They had us stack arms, which was connecting a number of rifles together with their stacking swivels, forming a triangle as shown in picture 19. We were instructed to have the cartridge chambers open. When all rifles were properly stacked, SDI Beeson and JDI Chapman then kicked those stacks of rifles over into the loose sand, and then kicked sand over them and made sure that the barrels and cartridge chambers were filled with sand. And then, the cleaning began. Believe me when I tell you that cleaning one's rifle, the chamber, the barrel and the guts of it, of every grain of sand was extremely difficult. If one grain of sand was found in any recruit's rifle, the whole process was repeated. The rifles were again stacked with cartridge chambers open and the D.I.s kicked them over and insured they were covered and filled with sand, and the cleaning process began again.

As I recall, we had to go through this process two or three times before the D.I.s were satisfied. The recruit whose rifle had that spot of rust was greatly relieved that he wasn't being sent to the brig. If he had been, the rest of us, having had to share the consequences of his offense, would probably have merrily sent him on his way.

As time progressed with the unending drill formations with the rifle, we became quite adept with the various "Manuel of Arms" movements while marching, such as right shoulder arms to left shoulder arms, left shoulder arms to right shoulder arms, port arms, order arms, trail arms, rifle salute, etc. But we never reached that point of perfection which was the D.I.s standard set for us, nor did we realize at the time that it was not possible to do so because it was unreachable, and the Marine way was to always give the maximum effort striving to reach that unreachable goal of perfection.

In addition to their supremely demanding responsibility of turning a bunch of ignorant civilian maggots into sharp Marines, the Drill Instructors had to put up with a frustrating situation that made their job more difficult. The Recruit Training Depot in San Diego was located adjacent to Lindberg International Airport, so the noise of airliners was almost always present. But that wasn't the main interruption. We were also located adjacent to Convair Aircraft Manufacturing Corporation, which built fighter jets for the Air Force. At the time, they were building the F-102 fighter interceptor for the Air Force. Noise from the airliners wasn't too bad, but the noise from those fighter jets was something else. The F-102 was equipped with the J-57 turbojet engine with afterburner, one of the most powerful jet engines at the time. Test flights were conducted almost daily, and when the pilots of those F-102s lit the afterburner on takeoff, the roar was deafening and reverberated throughout the area, drowning out all conversation, including commands given by the Drill Instructors to their marching troops, resulting in the D.I.'s profane comments regarding the pilot's genealogy.

Ten years later, as a Lieutenant, I was flying that jet as a combat ready F-102 fighter interceptor pilot in the Air Force.

Clothing on the bunk.

1

2

3

4

5

6

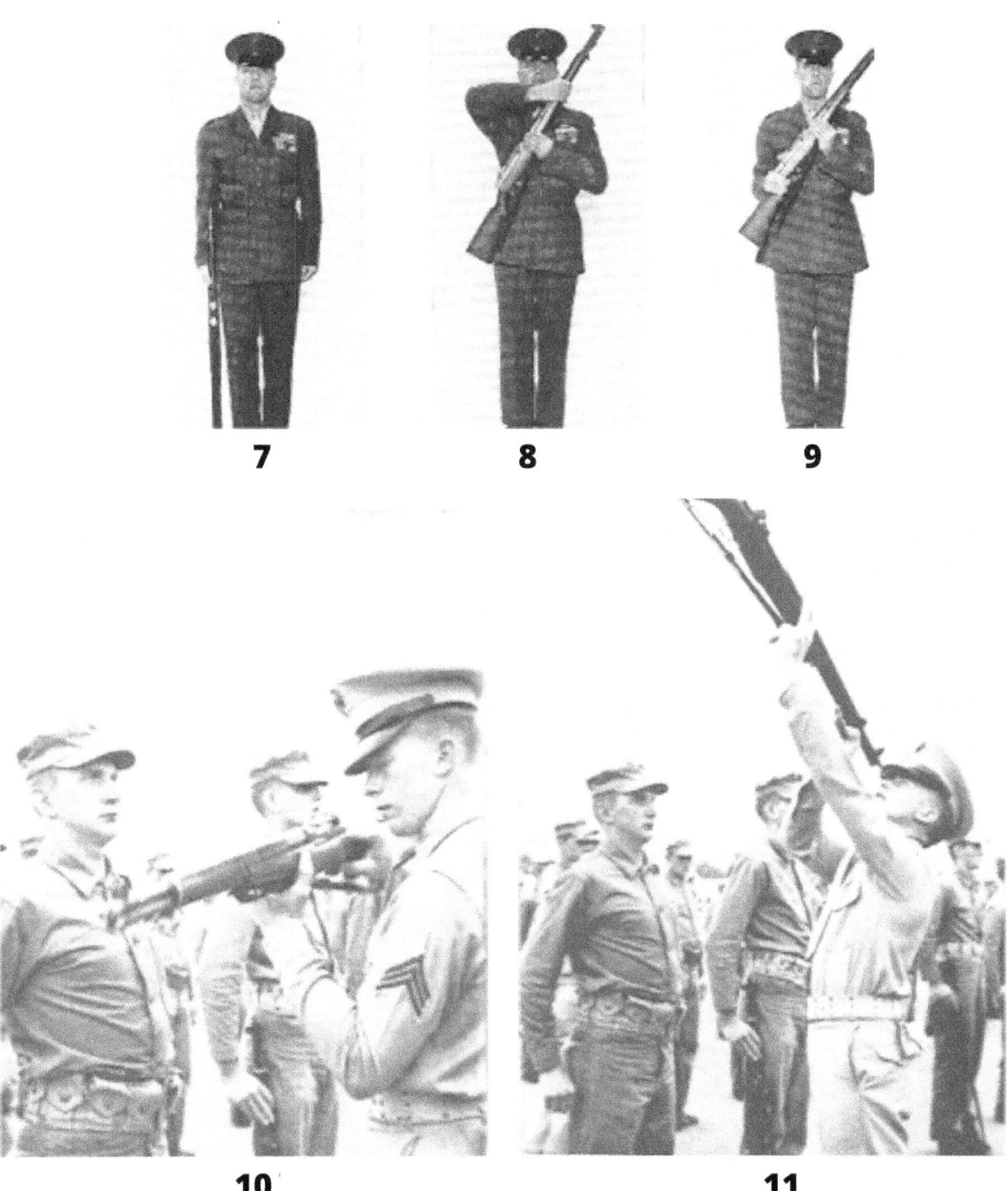

12 13 14 15

PORT ARMS TO ORDER ARMS. COMMAND: 1. Order 2. ARMS. (ONE) At the command ARMS, move the right hand from its grasp on the stock and regrasp the piece between the upper sling swivel and the stacking swivel. (TWO) Release the grasp of the left hand and lower the rifle to the right so that the butt is three (3) inches from the ground, barrel to the rear, left hand with fingers extended and joined steadying the rifle, forearm and wrist straight and inclining downward. (THREE) Complete the order by lowering the rifle gently to the ground with the right hand. Cut away the left hand smartly to the side.

16

17

18

19

*"Without discipline,
there is no Marine Corps."*

Gunny R. Lee Ermey

Chapter 11
The Marine Guard

Before I get to the subject of this chapter, I want to share a story concerning the brotherhood of arms. In the unit I was assigned to after boot camp and combat training, we had a member who had a serious speech impediment. When he started to speak, he would lose control. The volume of his speech would steadily increase to a shout, the tone of his speech would go higher and higher, the speed faster and faster, and the pronunciation more and more garbled until it was impossible to understand him. He was very self-conscious about this, and it was obvious that he had been on the receiving end of much criticism and even jokes about his disability in the past. I believe his name was Stan, and he was well-liked by the rest of us as a Marine brother. So, how did we handle it? Well, whenever it happened, we would say, "O.K. Stan, slow down, speak slower and not so loud and concentrate on pronouncing each word more clearly." And he would respond by forcing himself to regain control. The point is this: Stan knew he was safe with his fellow Marines from any embarrassment, criticism or jokes about his problem, and he need not feel self-conscious. He also knew that if any outsider or stranger gave him a hard time or messed with him, that person would have to deal with all of us, and it wouldn't be pretty. You mess with the Marine Brotherhood at your own peril. Back to the subject of this chapter.

One of the most important duties of a U.S. Marine is guard duty. Wherever a Marine is stationed, ashore or afloat aboard ship, at every Navy and Marine base worldwide, at all our embassies around the world, at Federal government installations, at shipyards and ammunition depots, not to mention Congress and the White House, a Marine Guard is established and maintained.

The Guard is charged with the preservation of order, protection of personnel and property, and the enforcement of orders and regulations. Each Marine Guard is supervised by an Officer of the Guard and either a Sergeant of the Guard or a Corporal of the Guard. Guard duty has been a function of special importance to Marines since the Corps was established, and this importance is drilled into the recruit from the time he enters boot camp until the time he leaves the Corps. During boot camp, we recruits were regularly scheduled for guard duty, guarding the boundaries and environs of our platoon area. Was this necessary for protection? No! Who would we protect against? Civilians trying to sneak into Marine boot camp? I don't think so! But it was absolutely necessary for training the recruit in the special duties and responsibilities of guard duty because, as I said, wherever he goes on assignment, he would be involved in guard duty in one form or another.

There are two types of orders for guard duty - Special Orders and General Orders. Special Orders are those pertaining to a particular post or location, or to unique duties associated with a specific tour of guard duty. General Orders do not change and are the same wherever Marines are located. There are 11 General Orders, and a Marine is required to memorize them and be able to recite them verbatim whenever he is called upon to do so. To give the reader some idea of a Marine Guard's responsibility, the 11 General Orders are listed below, with explanations where necessary. The orders themselves are in bold face, and these are what the Marine must memorize. It was, and I'm sure still is, common practice that, while a Marine was on guard duty, the Officer, Sergeant, or Corporal of the Guard would come to check that all was well, and while there, ask the guard to recite one or more of the General Orders. Woe to the guard if he couldn't do it, or if he hesitated and couldn't do it in a sharp, crisp, authoritative manner, leaving no doubt that he was in charge. The 11 General Orders are:

1. **To take charge of this post and all government property in view.**
   a. All persons in the military service, whether their rank be Private, General, or Admiral, are required to respect the guard in the performance of his duties as a sentry and member of the Guard.
2. **To walk my post in a military manner, keeping always on the alert, and observing everything that takes place within sight or hearing.**
3. **To report all violations of orders I am instructed to enforce.**
   a. If the case is urgent, and it is necessary, the guard is to apprehend the offender and call the Corporal of the Guard.
4. **To repeat all calls from posts more distant from the guardhouse than my own.**
   a. The guard is to pass on such calls from guards further from the guardhouse than he so that word will reach the Corporal of the Guard who will then act on the call as required.
5. **To quit my post only when properly relieved.**
   a. If the guard becomes sick, or for any reason must leave his post, he will call, "Corporal of the Guard, Post number ___, Relief!"
6. **To receive, obey, and pass on to the sentry who relieves me all orders from the commanding officer, officer of the day, and officers and noncommissioned officers of the guard only.**
   a. The guard is subject only to the orders of these officers during his tour of guard duty.
7. **To talk to no one except in the line of duty.**
   a. When persons make proper inquiries of you, answer courteously.
   b. If you are armed with a rifle when you are having conversation with any person, take the position of "port arms."
8. **To give the alarm in case of fire or disorder.**
   a. If the danger is great in case of either fire or disorder, and there is no other method of giving an immediate alarm, discharge your rifle or pistol three times in rapid succession before you call.
9. **To call the Corporal of the Guard in any case not covered by instructions.**
10. **To salute all officers, and all colors and standards not cased.**
    a. When you are a sentry, you salute all persons and parties entitled to this compliment. This includes officers of the Army, Navy, Marine Corps, Air Force, and Coast Guard. It also includes officers of the National Guard and Organized Reserves who are in uniform, and military and naval officers of friendly foreign powers.

b. When the flag is raised at morning colors or lowered at evening colors, the guard stands at attention at the first note of the National Anthem and renders the prescribed salute. If the guard is engaged in some duty which would be hampered, he needs not salute. When the music sounds "Carry On," the guard resumes regular duties.
11. **To be especially watchful at night and, during the time for challenging, to challenge all persons on or near my post, and to allow no one to pass without proper authority.**
   a. During challenging hours (times of heightened security), if a sentry sees any person or party on or near his post, he will advance quickly along his post toward such person or party, and when within 30 paces, he will challenge sharply with, "HALT! WHO IS THERE!" The sentry ordinarily continues to advance while challenging, but he may halt if circumstances require.
   b. The sentry will permit only one person of a party to approach him for the purpose of being duly recognized.
   c. A sentry may challenge any person or party whom he considers suspicious.

These are the 11 General Orders which every Marine must commit to memory and recite if asked. I have no doubt that if you asked the Commandant of the Marine Corps to recite the General Orders, he would remember them from his younger days.

Again, I emphasize the importance Marines attach to guard duty. I will give one example of this. After boot camp, during my tour as a radio operator in an artillery battalion, we boarded a huge troopship for maneuvers culminating in an amphibious landing on the beach near Camp Pendleton, Calif. In the bottom of that troopship, below the water line, was a huge room with bunks that were not being used and the room was locked up. Our commander convinced the Navy to unlock that room and make it available to us for guard duty. There we were, each of us having our turn of rotation for guarding an empty room not being used, and nearly getting knocked off our feet with every wave that struck the bottom of that ship, while we could have been laying on the deck sunning ourselves, smoking, or playing poker or rolling dice. No way, however, since the Marines never lost an opportunity for guard duty.

I'll end this discussion of the subject with this piece of advice: Don't ever mess with a Marine on guard duty, or you will suffer disastrous effects to bodily health and/or lifetime longevity.

"A ship without Marines is like a garment without buttons."

Admiral David D. Porter
USN, 1863

Chapter 12
First-Aid Classes

First-Aid refers to the medical procedures a Marine can carry out for himself or for his companions before emergency treatment can be given by a doctor or corpsman. The corpsmen can't be everywhere at once. There may be times when the Marine will have to depend on his own knowledge to save his own life or that of his buddy. And he can do that if he knows what to do and what not to do, and if he acts quickly and calmly. The first-aid classes are designed to teach the recruit just that.

Additionally, the recruit is taught that, as a Marine in combat, he can't stop to give help in the heat of battle. If he stops to aid someone who is wounded, there are two Marines out of the fight. By continuing to fight, he makes it possible for the corpsman to advance with the troops and give emergency treatment to the wounded. The Marine rifleman's first job is to fight.

During the classes, we were exposed to photos and films of wounds ranging from gunshot wounds to broken bones to some pretty ghastly injuries from mortar and artillery fire. The following is presented to give the reader some idea of what the recruit was required to learn. Pictures 1, 2, and 3 at the end depict typical classes.

We were first required to memorize the three steps for saving life. These are: 1. <u>Stop the bleeding</u>; 2. <u>Protect the wound from infection</u>; and 3. <u>Prevent or treat shock</u>. We were instructed in the simple methods for carrying out these three steps. As an aside, one could conclude that everyone should know these three steps, whether military or civilian. For example: You are first on the scene of a serious car accident, and an occupant of the car is bleeding profusely. If you know what to do, you will probably save a life. If you don't, you won't. Let's review these steps which we recruits had to learn in detail. Remember, this presupposes a combat environment.

First, to <u>stop the bleeding</u>, place a first-aid dressing from the first-aid kit over the wound and press hard. Use the wounded man's dressing because you may need your own later. If the wound is a large one, use two dressings because it is vitally important that the entire wound be covered completely. Place your hands over both dressings and spread pressure over the entire wound. Bleeding may not stop the instant you apply pressure, so keep it firm and continuous until it does stop, or you are sure it isn't going to stop.

We learned all about tourniquets, when to apply them and how to apply them. When pressure on the wound, or in the case of an arm or a leg, elevation of the wound, fails to stop the bleeding and blood is gushing from the wound, a tourniquet should be quickly applied. The tourniquet should always be placed above the wound, and if possible, the skin protected by placing it over the sleeve or trouser leg. Once in place, a tag should be attached to the individual indicating what time the tourniquet was applied. Tourniquets should be loosened every 30 minutes to allow fresh blood to get to all parts of the wounded area. The items needed to make a tourniquet and the steps for applying it are shown in pictures 4, 5, 6, and 7.

First, make a loop around the limb with a strip of cloth, a belt, or some such item. Second, pass a stick, scabbard, or bayonet under the loop. Third, tighten the loop just enough to stop the bleeding. And fourth, bind the free end to the person's limb in order to keep the tourniquet from unwinding.

The second life-saving step is <u>protect the wound from infection</u>. The first-aid bandage in the Marine's first-aid kit is designed to protect wounds from the outside by keeping dirt and germs out. It is also designed to protect wounds from further injury. When placing this bandage on a wound, take care that you keep the side that goes next to the wound clean. When being told this, the thought going through my mind, and I'm sure the minds of the other recruits was, "How do you do this in a combat environment which is probably the most unsanitary imaginable?"

The third step in saving a life is to <u>prevent or treat shock</u>. We learned that shock is a condition of great weakness of the body and can result in death. It may occur with any kind of wound, and the worse the wound, the more likely shock will develop. Severe bleeding causes shock. Also, a person in shock may tremble and appear nervous; he may be very pale, wet with sweat, and may lose consciousness. Shock may not occur for some time after an injury; therefore, we were told that in combat, every wounded man should be treated for shock before he has a chance to go into shock, and we were taught how to do this as follows:

1. Make the person comfortable. Take off his pack and anything else he is carrying. Loosen his belt and his clothes. Handle him very gently.
2. Do not move him more than absolutely necessary. If he is laying in a doubled up position, make sure no bones are broken before you straighten him out.
3. Lower his head and shoulders to increase the flow of blood to the brain. If the ground slants, turn him gently so that his feet are uphill and his head downhill. If he is unconscious, place him face down with his head turned to one side in case he should vomit.
4. Keep him warm with a blanket or coat. Place something under him to protect him.
5. Morphine will help prevent shock; however, if the person is unconscious, morphine should not be given.

It was emphasized that those three rules for saving lives, stop the bleeding, prevent infection, and prevent or treat shock, apply to the treatment of all wounds. However, there are certain types of wounds which require special first-aid measures. These types of wounds are chest wounds, belly wounds, jaw and face wounds, burns, and fractures. The *Guidebook for Marines*, which every recruit receives and must thoroughly digest, has extensive instructions for these special first-aid measures and medical treatment. I'll summarize each to give the reader an idea of how extensive they are, although some of it is a bit gruesome. And again, in my opinion, first-aid courses similar to those taught to Marine recruits should be required courses in high schools.

<u>Chest wounds</u>, through which air is being sucked in and blown out are particularly dangerous. The air squeezes and compresses the lung and prevents proper breathing. The wound must quickly be made air-tight with a dressing large enough to cover the entire wound and packed firmly to stop the flow of air. The dressing should then be covered with a larger piece of material and bound securely around the individual with belts, strips of torn clothing, or whatever is available to keep the wound airtight. If the wounded person wishes, let him sit up, since this may ease his breathing.

Belly wounds should also be covered with a sterile dressing and fastened securely. Again, treat the victim for shock. Do not try to replace or reposition any organs protruding from the victim's belly. To do so will cause both infection and severe shock. Do not give food or water to the victim. Anything taken by mouth will pass out from the intestine and spread germs through the belly.

Wounds to the face and neck need special treatment to avoid choking on blood. Also, bleeding from the face and the neck is usually severe because of the many blood vessels. First, stop the bleeding by exerting pressure with a sterile dressing, as shown in picture 8. Then bind the dressing to protect the wound.

If the wound is to the jaw, and the jaw is broken, tie the bandage around it and up over the head, as shown in picture 9 in order to give support. Ensure that you do not prevent the blood from draining out of the mouth. To insure against choking on blood, have the victim sit up with his head held forward and down, or lie face down. These positions will allow the blood to drain from his mouth instead of going down his windpipe.

Severe burns are quite likely to cause shock. Also, with burns, there is a great danger of infection. Do not pull clothing away from the burned area. Instead, cut or tear the clothing and gently lift it off the burned area. Don't try to remove pieces of cloth that stick to the skin of the burned area. If a medical kit containing burn ointment is available, apply ointment to the burn. Carefully cover the burned area with sterile dressings. Do not break blisters or touch the burn. Treatment for shock is especially important. Give the victim lots of water to drink because burns cause a great loss of body fluids. There is also a great loss of body salts. Therefore, if able, add two salt tablets or a 1/4 teaspoonful of loose salt to each canteen full of water, and three or more canteens of water should be drunk in 24 hours.

Fractures: We had to learn the four signs of a broken bone. These are: 1. Tenderness over the bone with pain on movement. 2. Inability to move injured part. 3. Unnatural shape or deformity. 4. Swelling and discoloration. However, a fracture may or may not have all these signs. If unsure, give the wounded man the benefit of the doubt and treat the injury as a fracture.

There are two main types of fractures - a simple break in the bone, and a broken bone with a wound from the outside, or a compound fracture (see pictures 10 and 11). The compound fracture can be caused by a broken bone piercing the skin or by a bullet which pierces the flesh and breaks the bone. Fractures usually require splinting which prevents the jagged edges of the bone from tearing blood vessels and nerves. In simple fractures, proper application of a splint will prevent the bone from piercing the skin, which would make it a compound fracture. On the other hand, if the fracture is compound, splinting it will prevent further injury to the wound and the introduction of more infection.

Proper splinting of the fracture greatly relieves the pain of a fracture and will reduce, and sometimes actually prevent shock. Additionally, if possible, all fractures of long bones should be splinted where the individual is before moving or transporting him to another location. The cracked ends of the bone are razor sharp and can cut through muscle, blood vessels, nerves, and skin.

Standard leg and arm splints are the most desirable when available; however, first-aid in the field may require the improvisation of splints from any material that is handy. Temporary splints can be made from boards, branches, poles, bayonets, scabbards, and so on. Splints should always be padded, if possible, with some soft material to protect the limb from pressure and rubbing. The splints should be bound securely at several places above and below the fracture, but not so tightly as to stop the flow of blood. For binding, one can use normal belts, cartridge belts, strips of cloth, handkerchiefs tied together, etc. It is well to apply two splints, one on either side of the limb. If the injured elbow is bent, do not try to straighten it . If straight, do not bend it. See picture 12 for various types of splints.

Broken back: Be wary of any back injury, especially if the back has been sharply struck or bent, or the person has fallen, since it is often impossible to be sure whether or not a man has a broken back. If the injured man's back is broken, there is the danger that the sharp bone fragments will cut the spinal cord if the man is moved. This would cause permanent paralysis of the body and legs. Don't move the victim unless absolutely necessary, and don't raise his head or twist his neck or back. Place a rolled blanket or other similar item under his back for support.

Broken neck: A broken neck is extremely dangerous. Bone fragments may cut the spinal cord just as in a broken back. Keep the head straight and still since moving it may cause death. Place a rolled blanket around the head and neck for support and padding. To keep the head and neck motionless, large stones or backpacks can be placed on each side of the head as shown in picture 13. If the victim must be moved, get help. One person supports the man's head and keeps it straight while others lift him and put him on a hard stretcher or board. If the wounded man is experiencing severe pain, morphine should be given him. Morphine comes in small collapsible tubes. Morphine both relieves pain and helps to decrease shock. However, don't use morphine within two hours of a previous injection, or when a man is unconscious, when he has a head injury, or when he breathes less than 12 times a minute.

Care of the feet: For the Marine rifleman, this is all-important. Most of this is common sense, but it was emphasized. Why? Because on the battlefield it can be easily neglected. Keep feet clean as possible. Dry feet thoroughly after washing them, especially between the toes. Apply GI foot powder daily. Cutting a callous or corn risks serious infection. To avoid ingrown toenails, keep toenails clean and short, and cut them straight across. Dust feet with GI foot powder before a march. Foot powder absorbs perspiration and prevents chafing. Put on clean socks every day if possible, and break in shoes and boots before wearing them on a march.

Snakebite: For poisonous snakebite, giving first-aid immediately is the most important thing to do. Then, if possible, kill and keep the snake so that it can be identified, and proper medicine given by a medical officer. The person bitten should remain as quiet as possible and not walk or run about. If the bite is on the arm or leg, improvise a tourniquet and apply it between the bite and the heart, above the elbow or knee joint. The tourniquet must be tight enough to stop the flow of blood returning to the heart.

Next, make a crosscut over each fang mark long enough and deep enough to allow free bleeding - about 1/4 inch long and 1/4 inch deep. Suck the poison from the wound, spitting it out frequently. Snake poison is harmless in the mouth unless there are cuts through which the poison can get into the blood, a fact that most of us were unaware of. Suction should be kept on the wound for at least one hour; however, the tourniquet must be loosened every thirty minutes for a few seconds to allow fresh blood to flow to all parts of the injured person.

A snakebite victim can do all these things for himself if he is able to reach the wound with his mouth. If the bite is on a part of the body where a tourniquet cannot be applied, make the cross-cut incisions and apply suction just the same. After first-aid, secure medical help as soon as possible.

There were many other aspects of first-aid covered in these classes such as effects of heat and cold, artificial respiration, transportation of the sick and wounded, but those given here should give the reader some knowledge of the extent and quality of the training the recruit received.

> *"I have only two out of my company and twenty out of some other company. We need support, but it is almost suicide to try to get it here as we are swept by machine gun fire and a constant barrage is on us. I have no one on my left and only a few on my right. I WILL HOLD."*
>
> *1st Lt. Clifton B. Cates, USMC, 96th Co.*
> *Soissons, 19 July 1918*

1

2

3

4

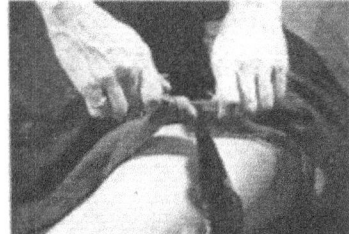

Make loop around limb.

5

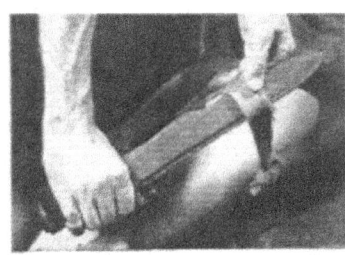

Pass stick or scabbard under loop.

6

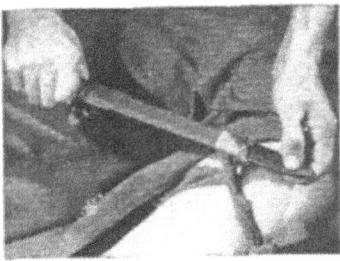

Tighten loop until bleeding stops.

7

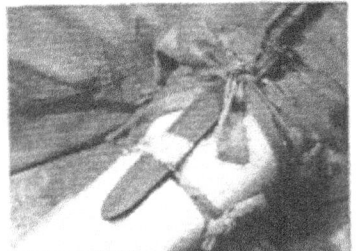

Bind stick to the limb.

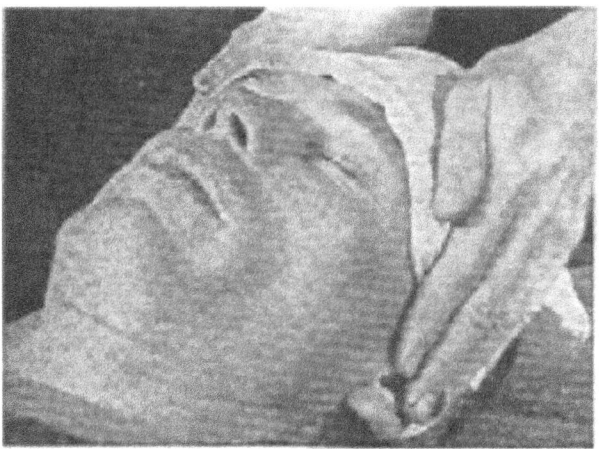

Using pressure to stop bleeding.

8

Protecting and supporting jaw wound

9

Upper left, splint for broken leg or thigh; upper right, splint for arm fracture where elbow can't be bent; lower left, splint for fracture of lower arm; lower right, splint for fracture of upper arm.

12

10

Simple fracture.

Compound fracture.

11

Protection for broken neck.

13

Chapter 13
Physical Training

To refer to Marine boot camp as physically demanding would be a gross understatement. As I previously mentioned, we had the constant drill, drill, and more drill, and if we weren't marching, we were running, both around the two-mile parade field, and in normal movement from one location to another where walking would be the normal means of conveyance. And then we had the other physical exercises as shown in the pictures shown at the end of the chapter. Notice that in pictures 1 and 2 the M-1 rifle is incorporated into the exercise. This was common. I previously referred to the M-1 rifle as the Marine's companion. This was not said in jest. After being issued our rifles, it became like another appendage to our bodies. It was with us during drill formation, during physical exercise, and during unending hours of cleaning it, polishing it, disassembling it, and reassembling it. Thinking back on it, I am surprised that the Drill Instructors didn't have us sleeping with it.

The Drill Instructors wanted our rifles, along with our boots, shoes, belt buckles, and other uniform brass to "shine like a diamond in a goat's ass." Don't ask me to explain the meaning of that phrase. I have no idea. It was just a favorite saying of the Drill Instructors to describe their standard of perfection.

Notice also on the picture page of this chapter picture 3 of recruits doing pushups. This was an activity that we became thoroughly familiar with since pushups were one of the primary means of incentive used by the Drill Instructors to get us recruits to try harder to meet the standard of performance demanded by them. And it was rare, extremely rare, almost to the point of non-existence, that a Drill Instructor would concede that a recruit had met Marine standards in any activity or event until the final week of so of boot camp. So, invariably, pushups to the point of exhaustion, and then a few more, would be the recruit's lot.

At the beginning of boot camp, some of my fellow recruits, especially those carrying extra weight, had a hard time doing pushups. At the end of boot camp, pushups were as effortless to them, as to the rest of us, as walking, running, or breathing. As for myself, during life after my time in the Marines, whenever I felt guilty about avoiding exercise, I would remember boot camp and take up a regimen of pushups as my primary exercise. When I was in my fifties and sixties, I could still get down and do 50 pushups with minimal exhaustion afterwards.

An important part of our physical exercise was running the obstacle course as shown in the pictures. Of course, the Drill Instructors had demanding time and performance standards we had to meet for this also. As time passed, most of the platoon either met or came close to meeting those standards. Again, our fellow recruits who were on the heavy side had problems on the monkey bars shown in picture 4. Also, hand walking the bars shown in picture 5 was demanding.

Walking on the ropes, as shown in picture 6 was a challenge to one's balance, as was walking on the logs shown in picture 7. The wall, shown in picture 8 was just high enough to make it very difficult to scale. Most of us failed on the first try and some had to try three or four times before they succeeded. Of course, the Drill Instructors would not allow anyone to give up. Everyone was going to scale that wall, no matter how long or how many attempts it took.

Here was another insight into the Drill Instructors' strategy for building a Marine. When a recruit was ready to give up on himself to accomplish a tough task, the Drill Instructors were not. They forced the recruit, by insults, threats, or whatever, to keep trying until they were successful. Because of this, we recruits developed a new standard of what we were capable of, physically and mentally. And that standard kept increasing not only throughout boot camp, but during our entire time in the Corps. And for those who left the Corps after their tour of duty, that standard of performance went with them back to civilian life and their chosen work career. I suspect that is the reason employers prefer to hire veterans as employees.

Other physical challenges offered by the obstacle course are shown in pictures 9 and 10. The recruits swinging on ropes in picture 11 are trying to make it past a pit filled with muddy water. Failure to make it past and land on dry land results in a muddy bath. Descending a rope ladder, shown in picture 12, simulated climbing down the side of a troopship into a landing craft for an amphibious landing. Amphibious warfare was the Marines' primary combat mission at the time. We quickly learned one important lesson in using a rope ladder. When climbing down, grab the vertical portions of the rope with your hands, and not the horizontal segments, since the horizontal segments are where the person following you is placing his boots.

I learned another lesson concerning rope ladders over a year later while participating in an actual amphibious landing. It's a long, long, way down from the deck of that troopship to the landing craft in the water below. It's best not to look down until you are near the water. Also, the correct timing of one's release of the rope ladder and stepping into the boat is critical. That landing craft is rising up and down with the waves, and if the waves are down, the distance between the rope ladder and the landing craft is considerable. If you release the rope ladder when the landing craft is beginning its downward cycle, you're going to have quite a fall, and loaded down with your combat gear, it will be a nasty one. The trick is to wait until the landing craft begins its upward wave cycle, and then as it crests, release the rope ladder and step into the boat. Of course, Marines already in the landing craft help their buddies get into the boat.

Finally, in addition to all this physical exercise and training, there was the physical activity of the weekly field day. Great emphasis was placed on cleanliness and sanitation. I've already mentioned the laundry procedures. With forty recruits bunked close together in each quonset hut, it goes without saying that cleanliness and sanitation was paramount. Thus, the weekly field day, which involved cleaning of the barracks.

The foot lockers would be placed on the bunks, the concrete floors of the barracks hosed down with water, and then buckets we had filled with sand would be emptied on the wet floor and then spread to cover the whole floor. Then we recruits, with hand brushes with stiff bristles, would, on our hands and knees, scrub that concrete floor until it was as clean and sanitized as a concrete floor could possibly be. A scrubbing with long-handled scrub brushes followed and the sand was removed. Finally, the floor was mopped dry. When finished, I, as Right Guide, would inform the Drill Instructors that the barracks were ready for inspection.

The Drill Instructors were, of course, thorough in their inspection, particularly in the areas underneath the wall lockers and around the legs of the bottom bunks. What they were looking for was any residue of sand which was easy to miss when we were cleaning the floor. If they found any, you guessed it, we had to hose the floor down again and mop it dry. In cleaning the "head," our bathroom and shower facilities, we used toothbrushes to clean around the bases of the faucets, spigots, and toilet bowls to insure there was no dirt in the joints and seams. You may ask, "Who cleaned the Drill Instructors' living, bathroom, and shower facilities?" Silly question! Obviously, we recruits did. And here too, our first effort rarely passed their inspection, and we would end up doing the whole thing over again.

I'll end this chapter with a description of an event we recruits participated in called the "Recruits' Midnight Requisition Mission." In order to do all the cleaning of the facilities mentioned in the foregoing, each platoon of recruits was issued a supply of brooms, mops, hand brushes, long-handled scrub brushes and other cleaning materials. These items were kept neatly in a rack outside the platoon's quonset huts. They were prized items and every platoon wanted to have more of them, because the more you had, the more recruits could be working together doing the cleaning at the same time, instead of having to organize a number of work shifts so all members were involved in the task. This would allow field day cleaning requirements to be completed faster and more efficiently. Each platoon of recruits was therefore anxious to increase their store of these items, with priority given to mops and long-handled scrub brushes.

Over time, this desire led to a tradition referred to above as the "Recruits' Midnight Requisition Mission." This mission involved two recruits, chosen by lot as I recall, sneaking off after midnight to another recruit platoon's area and making off with a few (not many, just a few) of their cleaning utensils. If the recruits could get away with a mop and a long-handled scrub brush, the midnight requisition mission was a resounding success. As I said, we would only take one or two items. After all, our victims were fellow recruits who were doing the same thing, so we adhered to an "honor among thieves" code.

The Drill Instructors condoned this; in fact, they encouraged it. They informed us, early on, that if any recruits from another platoon managed to midnight requisition any of our cleaning items, they expected us to react accordingly to replace them, and not delay in doing so. I mentioned earlier that we recruits pulled individual shifts of guard duty over the platoon area at night. We kept our eyes open for any midnight requisitioners, but we couldn't isolate ourselves to the area where the cleaning supplies were located. We had the whole platoon area to patrol.

Nevertheless, if recruits from another platoon were successful in their midnight requisition of any of our supplies, the guard on duty suffered serious embarrassment. And so, although the loss involved only a couple of cleaning utensils, the Drill Instructors could use it to emphasize the critical importance the Corps associated with "heads-up" guard duty. Also, a successful recruit midnight requisition mission involved expertise in applying the use of "night reconnaissance procedures" taught in the classroom to the mission as follows: Avoid open spaces and lighted areas; stay in the dark shadows of the quonset barracks; carefully observe the movements of the platoon's guard on duty and identify and time those movements when he is not in a position to see you; choose such a time and make your raid on the other platoon's supplies swift and effective, grabbing only a couple items and then retreating back into the shadows and darkness; finally, make your way back to your platoon area with stealth and extreme caution.

One last item regarding the Recruit Midnight Requisition Mission. When choosing a recruit platoon to raid, don't choose the one located next to your platoon. Their deficit of supplies and your surplus will be quickly noticed, along with your identity as the thief. Choose a platoon further away with whom your platoon has little or no interaction to better mask your guilt.

Looking back over it all, I came to realize that during that time in Marine boot camp, we recruits were living the healthiest lifestyle of any we lived before and probably since. In addition to all the physical training and activity mentioned in this chapter, we were up at 5:00 a.m. every morning, in bed at 9:00 p.m. every night, providing eight hours of solid sleep, and receiving three healthy and substantial meals a day. Additionally, the smokers in the platoon experienced a substantial decrease in how often they were allowed to smoke, thereby contributing to the healthy lifestyle.

All of us were in the best physical shape of our lives after boot camp. I mentioned that I entered boot camp weighing around 125 pounds, and when I graduated after those 12 weeks, I was a solid 140 pounds. When I went home on 10 days leave after boot camp, my family and friends were astounded at the change. So much for their previous comments that I wasn't physically capable of becoming a Marine.

I can't resist adding a further comment before I close the chapter. On the train heading home on leave after boot camp, I was in my tan uniform. Other service members, Army, Navy, and Air Force were on the train. A nice-looking lady, in her late thirties or early forties, came up to me and said, "I just want you to know that you are the sharpest, most impressive military member on this train." My response was, "Thank you ma'am, I'm a Marine," as if to say, "Being the sharpest, most impressive, is only normal for a U.S. Marine."

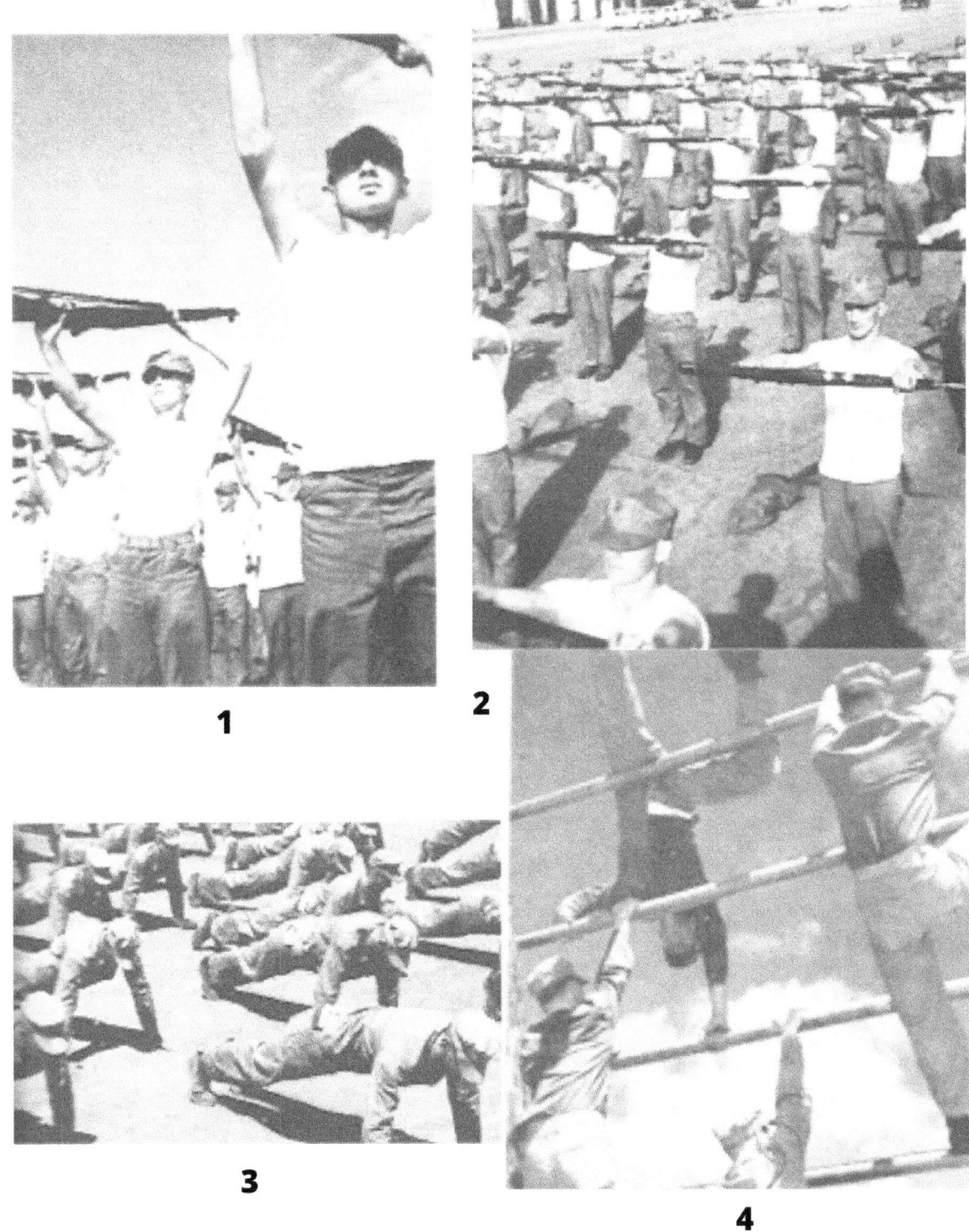

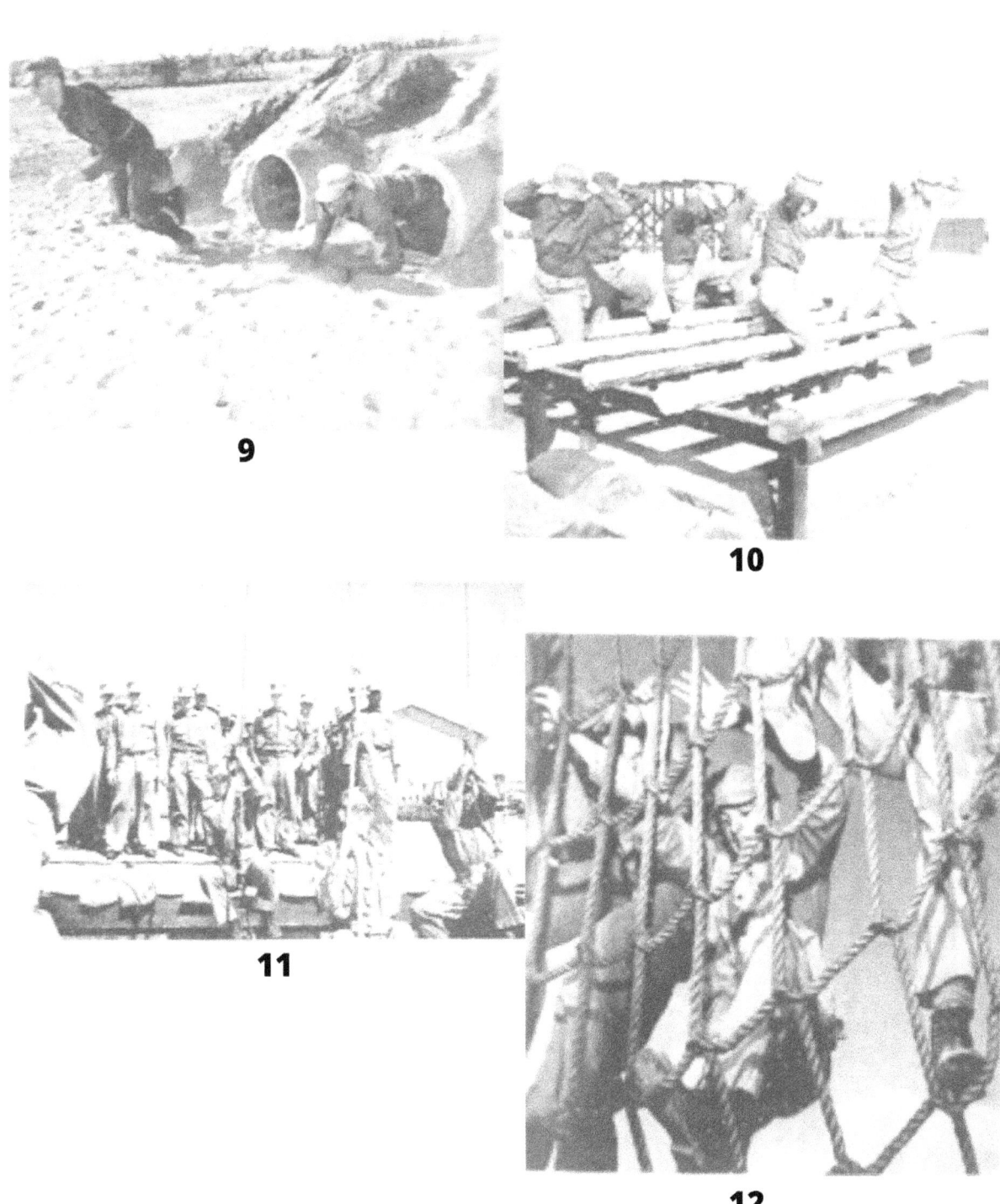

9

10

11

12

*"A Marine is a Marine.
There is no such thing as a former Marine.
You're just in different uniform and you're
in a different phase of your life. But you will
always be a Marine because you went to
Parris Island, San Diego, or the hills of Quantico.
There is no such thing as a former Marine."*

General James F. Amos
35th Commandant of the Marine Corps

Chapter 14
Camp Matthews Rifle Range
(Part 1)

We were nearly at the halfway point through boot camp, and it was time to head for the Marine Rifle Range at Camp Matthews, approximately 30 miles north of San Diego. It was there that we would conduct the most important training of our time in boot camp, and each of us strive to achieve the most important personal goal of boot camp - rifle qualification. The importance of this could not be overstated. Remember my previous comment that "every Marine, regardless of job specialty, was first and foremost a rifleman." Therefore, if the combat situation required it, Marines in the rear area, whether mechanic, cook, truck driver, etc., would take their rifle and join their comrades in the firing line. That rifle qualification badge was the first award the Marine received and was displayed prominently on his uniform with other ribbons of medals he would receive during his time in the Corps.

We boarded the buses for the trip up the coast to Camp Matthews which was something of a treat for all of us. We had been confined to the recruit area of the base at San Diego with little or no contact with the outside world for six weeks. That bus ride gave us a taste, although minuscule, of freedom, not to mention the beautiful scenery and glimpses of the vast Pacific Ocean on the way. And consider this. The year was 1956 and the landscape with its rolling hills was vastly different from what it is today after more than sixty years of commercial and residential development eroding much of that natural beauty.

On the way, we passed Miramar Naval Air Station, and the jet fighters were in the traffic pattern practicing landings close to our position on the highway. This was especially enjoyable to me because of my overriding ambition to become a fighter pilot, and my hope that the Marines would be the door of opportunity for me to achieve that ambition was always uppermost in my mind.

Our tenure at Camp Matthews would be three weeks, the second week filled with everything there is to know about the M-1 Garand Rifle, training and practicing with the weapon far beyond anything we had done thus far, and finally, during the third week, firing the course for qualification and hoping and praying that we did qualify, for failing to do so, entailed being saddled with a stigma that one wanted to avoid at all costs. But before starting that second week of rifle training and practice qualification, our first week of duty at Camp Matthews entailed mess duty - working in the mess hall from sunup to sundown.

At any one time, there were a number of recruit platoons at Camp Matthews undergoing rifle training and qualification, and they all had spent their first week there doing mess duty and hating it. Now it was our turn to spend a week on mess duty and hate it. Why hate it? Along with the long, long hours, it was a messy job (pardon the pun) surrounded by piles of food scraps, piles of dirty dishes, piles of dirty utensils, and piles of dirty food trays, left by hundreds of recruit trainees.

We recruits accomplished the various duties assigned to us on a rotational basis from meal to meal. Some of those duties are shown in the pictures included. Picture 1 shows recruits chopping heads of lettuce. Instead of lettuce, you could substitute cantaloupe, watermelon, or any other food item that needs chopping. Notice that the recruits aren't wearing gloves, aprons, or any other sanitary clothing items that are worn today. Picture 2 shows one of the permanent staff workers dressed in white instructing recruits on the fine art of peeling potatoes. It took a bit of practice to become proficient at peeling a potato without having a goodly portion of the potato being thrown away with the peeling. Notice the bags of potatoes stacked against the wall. With multiple recruit platoons undergoing training at Camp Matthews, hundreds of recruits were being fed at each meal. Again, notice that the recruits aren't wearing gloves, aprons, or any other sanitary clothing.

Picture 3 on the left shows a recruit stirring something in a huge vat. That something is probably mashed potatoes, since it took that vat, and probably more, of mashed potatoes to serve the number of recruits at each meal. Again, no sanitary gloves, aprons, or clothing.

Picture 4 to the right shows recruits taking their turn working on the serving line. Here they are in their t-shirts with no sanitary gloves, apron, etc., and like in the previous illustrations, wearing their standard Marine covers instead of sanitary skullcaps. There were occasional arguments and fights breaking out on the serving line. You had recruits from one platoon being served by recruits from another platoon, and the spirit of competition sometimes resulted in insults being exchanged which could easily get out of control.

Also, recruits on the serving line were instructed by permanent staff on how large a portion of each food item a recruit going through the line was to receive. It was common for the recruits to ask the server for an extra portion of one item or another. How the recruit serving the food handled this could result in either a confrontation or the line continuing to move uninterrupted. Normally, the recruit server would give the requestor an extra portion if there were no permanent staff around and he could do so without being seen.

Picture 5 to the left shows recruits washing the big serving trays. It doesn't show the mountain of dirty dishes, utensils, pots and pans left for the recruits to clean after every meal serving hundreds of recruits. And it was all done with bare hands without sanitary gloves or other items. Dishwashers were not available. This was perhaps the messiest of the messy jobs associated with mess duty, and we were glad when our rotation as dishwashers was behind us.

Picture 6 to the right shows recruits scrubbing the mess hall floor. After every meal was finished, preparation for the next meal began. This included scrubbing down the mess hall. Cleanliness and sanitation of the mess hall were absolutely mandatory, and after serving meals to hundreds of recruits three times a day, the mess hall floor, tables, chairs, and serving line had to be scrubbed and sanitized three times a day. That unenviable task, of course, fell to us recruit laborers.

Well, we all drew an immense sigh of relief when our week of mess duty was completed. Although it was a totally forgetful experience, there was one event that occurred that I cannot forget and which was indelibly imprinted on my mind. It occurred on the day I was assigned the duty of acquiring the signature of each Drill Instructor on a registration sheet when they brought their platoon to the mess hall.

This duty was also rotated among the recruits, and was highly desired since it meant that the recruit could spend much of the time that day outside waiting on the Drill Instructors instead of working inside the mess hall.

The Drill Instructors would march their platoons up to the mess hall door, and either call them to a halt, or command "Mark Time," which would have them marching in place. Once he called them to a "halt," the recruit would approach him and with a "Sir! request your signature on the registration sheet, Sir!" hand him the sheet and pen. After signing, he would direct his recruits to proceed single file into the mess hall. The recruit would remain at attention until the Drill Instructor had entered the mess hall.

The event that made that indelible impression on my mind involved a Drill Instructor who had a reputation for being a real badass. Before becoming a Marine and a Drill Instructor, he had been an Army paratrooper. He was also an Arnold Schwarzenegger before there was an Arnold Schwarzenegger. Even his muscles had muscles, and he was also known as an expert in martial arts.

As he was marching his platoon to the mess hall, I noticed that he was on the opposite side of his recruits than I was. I would have to cross over to his side of the platoon to get his signature on the registration form. And so, at a distance in front of his platoon, and while he was marching them, I crossed over in front of them to the side where he was. Big, big, mistake!

Remember in a previous chapter where I mentioned some of the dos and don'ts of a recruit in basic training. One of those don'ts was to never cross in front of a Drill Instructor marching his platoon except at a very, very, long distance. Well, this was not a very, very, long distance, and I had violated that rule.

That Drill Instructor immediately called his platoon to a halt and headed straight for me like an Abrams tank ready to crush whatever was in its way. I knew immediately what I had done, and as the realization dawned on me, my heart sank down to toe level and I was filled with fear - no, let's make that terror. He came up to me, and without pause, gave me two, or was it three, hard judo chops to the throat which sent me reeling, choking and gasping, against the brick wall of the mess hall. He then took my head in his fist and banged it hard two, or was it three, times against that brick wall. Then, with his nose nearly touching mine, and those cold eyes staring into mine, he said, "You little xihwykis, if you ever again cross in front of my platoon while I'm marching them, I'll kill you!"

What was my response to that mean Drill Instructor? Well, I informed him that his treatment of me was in direct violation of the Uniform Code of Military Justice, that he had cruelly invaded my safe space and had severely damaged my self-esteem, and that I would be reporting him to higher authorities. Yeah, right! Remember this is 1956 and the term "safe spaces" had not yet been invented by the liberal establishment, nor had the term "self-esteem" entered the liberal lexicon. And even if they had, the Marine Corps would not have taken them seriously. And so, what was my response to that mean Drill Instructor? It was "YES SIR!" "YES SIR!" "YES SIR!"

There's an important distinction here. Today, and even back then, that Drill Instructor would undoubtedly be charged with a violation of the Uniform Code of Military Justice if a recruit reported such behavior to higher authorities. Back then, however, such behavior was unofficially accepted by higher authorities and the recruits themselves, as part of the learning, training, shaping, and forming of a United States Marine. The recruits took pride in having toughed it out and probably would not have had it any different if given a choice. As proof of this, ask any Marine to tell you of his time in boot camp, as I am doing in writing this. And so, I leave it up to the individual reader to decide whether such behavior was justified or not those many years ago, or even today.

With our distasteful week of mess duty over, we could now turn our attention to the primary reason we were at Camp Matthews - rifle qualification.

*"Old Breed? New Breed?
There's not a damn bit of difference
so long as it's the Marine Breed."*

Lt. Gen. Lewis "Chesty" Puller

1

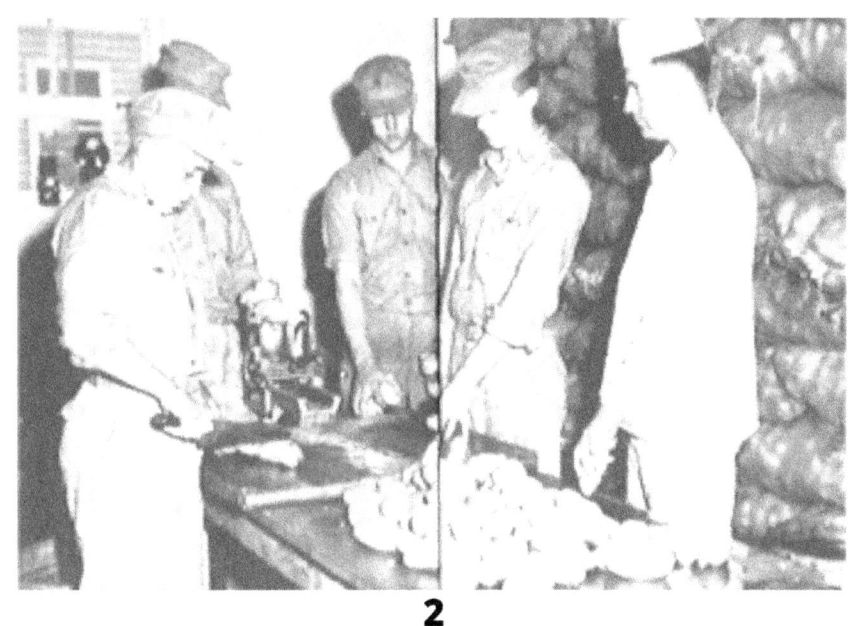

2

3

4

5

6

Chapter 15
Camp Matthews Rifle Range
(Part 2)

We were now about to engage in the most important training event in all of boot camp. Remember that I said earlier that every Marine, regardless of specialty, was first and foremost a rifleman. Therefore, rifle qualification was the most important of the recruit's accomplishments during basic training. It was also vitally important to the Drill Instructors because the greater the number of recruits in their platoon that qualified with the rifle, the more effective their duty performance as D.I.s was considered by their superiors. Therefore, during rifle qualification week, the Drill Instructors' attitude toward their recruits seemed to soften just a tiny bit and they almost became human. However, lest the reader misunderstand and place too much emphasis on this, the words "tiny" and "almost" are the operative words here.

Firing for qualification entailed firing 50 rounds from four posture positions, which I will describe later, from ranges of 200, 300, and 500 yards. Each round counted for 5 points if it was a bullseye, with corresponding lesser points depending on its distance from the bullseye. Thus, a maximum of 250 points was possible. At the time, the Marine Corps was the only branch of service that had its recruits shooting for qualification from as far away as 500 yards (1500 feet).

There were three levels of qualification available to the recruit. The lowest level was Rifle Marksman and required a minimum of 190 points to qualify as Marksman. The next highest level was Rifle Sharpshooter and required a minimum of 210 points to qualify as Sharpshooter. The highest level of qualification was Rifle Expert and required a minimum of 220 points to qualify as Expert. The corresponding qualification badges are shown in picture 1 on the first picture page.

SDI Beeson had informed me that, as his Right Guide of the platoon, he expected me to qualify as Expert. Nothing like a bit of pressure on this skinny little recruit who had fired a gun only two or three times in his life, and that had been his dad's shotgun.

All of us were just hoping and praying that we would at least qualify as Marksman, since we had seen other platoons who had finished qualification marching with a few recruits marching a distance from the rear of the platoon, shouting crude insults about themselves because they had not qualified with the rifle. None of us wanted that experience. I was glad to learn some years later that such degrading punishment had been discontinued, and that recruits who had failed to qualify with their platoon, would be sent back to another platoon to undergo rifle training and qualification all over again until they qualified. This, of course, delayed their graduation date, meaning more time in boot camp. I can't think of a greater incentive and motivator for a recruit to give a thousand percent effort to rifle qualification than the thought of delayed graduation and more time in boot camp.

The week of training prior to firing for qualification was called the snapping in period. It involved intense hours of study in the classroom and practice on the firing line, learning all there was to know about the M-1 Garand rifle, and practicing the four firing positions - standing, kneeling, sitting, and prone - to determine the most comfortable posture in each position for each recruit given their height, weight, and build. Along with this was finding the best adjustment of the rifle's ferrule, or shoulder strap, to hold the rifle perfectly steady while preparing to fire to avoid any tremor or movement. The Drill Instructors worked closely with other instructors in this preparation phase, sharing their experience and expertise, to give their recruits the best possible chance to qualify.

However, prior to commencing this intense period of preparation, we spent some time managing the targets and scoring for other platoons firing for record. An instructor described target information communicated to the shooter from the target area to assist the shooter in achieving his best score. This is shown in picture 2. The information included range elevation setting, wind direction, and wind velocity settings. There was a long line of targets that we would fire on as shown in picture 3. Obviously, it was critical for the recruit to fire on his assigned target in that line of targets. To insure this, he would count off the number of targets from the left to his assigned target before firing every round.

Picture 4 shows recruits preparing the targets and pictures 5 and 6 show them in the target pits marking hits on the target. The target is then raised so the scorekeeper can observe the hits and record them. All this is done under the watchful eyes of the Drill Instructors. We all enjoyed working in the target pits with the shells whizzing over our heads and scoring the hits. We gave a cheer when a round scored a bullseye, and when a round was outside the target boundaries at the target edges, we had a pole with a red flag on it, which we called Maggie's drawers, which we waved. But now it was time to get down to the serious business of qualifying as a Marine Rifleman.

As mentioned, we had had our rifles issued to us some time back, and along with the manual of arms, learned how to quickly disassemble them, clean them, and quickly reassemble them numerous times. But if we thought we knew all there was to know about that rifle, we were soon dissuaded of that notion. Whereas our disassembly of the rifle had consisted of the three major parts - the stock, the barrel, and the trigger housing, we were now to break down those three major components into their individual parts, become familiar with them, and fit them all together again. This was absolutely necessary. If the rifle malfunctioned in combat, it was essential that the Marine be able to diagnose the problem, and if possible, fix it on the battlefield. The following gives the reader an appreciation of what we had to learn, the majority of which comes from my 68 year old individual copy of Guidebook for Marines.

The M-1 rifle is a gas-operated, clip-fed, air-cooled, semi-automatic shoulder weapon. Its principal characteristic is its rapid mechanical operation which enables the individual rifleman, or a group of riflemen, to deliver a large volume of accurate fire upon any designated point or area. The rifle's effective range is 500 yards. Some of its characteristics are: Weight - 9.5 pounds; length without bayonet - 43.6 inches; average rate of aimed fire per minute - 30 rounds; muzzle velocity per second - 2600 - 2800 feet; magazine clip capacity - 8 rounds. We had to learn the nomenclature, that is, the names of all visible parts of the rifle as shown in picture 7.

As mentioned, we were already familiar with dissembling the rifle into its three major groups - the Stock Group, the Barrel and Receiver Group, and the Trigger Housing Group, as shown in picture 8. But now, we were to greatly increase our knowledge of the rifle by breaking down each of the three major groups into their component parts. I will not discuss the components of each major group, but only show illustrations of these components to give the reader an appreciation of the complexity of this outstanding battlefield weapon. Avid gun owners will probably enjoy this section. First, we have the M-1 Trigger Housing Group shown in picture 9. Next is the Barrel and Receiver Group in pictures 10 and 11, and finally the Stock Group in picture 12.

If you count the number of individual components in the three main rifle nomenclature groups, they will total around one hundred. Obviously, a Marine would not have all those components memorized; however, he had to be familiar with each, its operation, other part or parts it was connected to, and how to replace it. One may ask, "Where do you find replacement parts on the battlefield?" Answer: "From your dead comrades' weapons." One may ask, "Why not just use the rifle of a dead comrade and dispose of your own?" Answer: The serial number of your rifle, which you have memorized, is recorded with your name in official records, and you darn well better be able to account for it. If your rifle malfunctions during battle, you may well have to use a dead or wounded comrade's weapon, but you don't just throw your malfunctioning rifle away on the battlefield. You fix it when and if able or turn it in for a specialist to fix it and get a replacement.

Along with the nomenclature and inner components of the rifle, we learned the functioning of the rifle, what all happens when you pull that trigger, and that firing the M-1 rifle consists of basically two movements - the Rearward Movement which ejects the empty cartridge case and cocks the rifle, and the Forward Movement which puts a new cartridge into the chamber, ready to be fired. Understanding these movements was essential so that the Marine would know what to do if at any time his rifle failed to operate normally.

We had to know the individual steps involved in both the rearward and forward movements. For example: The Rearward Movement consists of four steps:

1. <u>Ignition.</u> The hammer strikes the firing pin and ignites the primer at the base of the cartridge as shown in picture 13. The bolt must be in a fully locked position before this can take place.

2. <u>Action of the gas.</u> When the bullet passes the gas port, as shown in picture 14, some of the gases escape into the gas chamber. The gases strike the piston with sufficient force to drive the operating rod to the rear, compressing the operating rod spring.

3. <u>Movement of the Operating Rod.</u> As the operating rod moves to the rear, it unlocks the bolt and carries it to the rear along with the empty cartridge, which is removed from the chamber by the extractor, as shown in picture 15. When the empty cartridge clears the mouth of the breech, the ejector throws the empty round to the right through the action of the compressed ejector spring as shown.

4. <u>Cocking of the Hammer.</u> As the bolt is carried to the rear, it rides over the hammer, forcing it back and compressing the hammer spring, thus cocking it, as shown in picture 16. At the same time, the follower arm forces another cartridge up in the clip as shown in picture 17. This terminates the Rearward Movement, and with the gases forcing the operating rod to the rear expended, the Forward Movement can commence.

The Forward Movement consists of the following two steps, actuated by the compressed operating rod spring.

1. With the bolt in its extreme rearward position, the top cartridge in the clip is uncovered, as mentioned. Then, as the compressed operating rod spring moves the bolt forward, the lower front face of the bolt contacts the base of the top cartridge of the clip, sliding it forward into the chamber.

2. As the operating rod moves the bolt forward, the bolt is rotated clockwise, engaging the locking lugs which lock the bolt in position. This terminates the Forward Movement and the rifle is ready to fire again.

We were instructed in various stoppages that might occur and immediate actions that can be taken in a combat situation to resolve those stoppages. The stoppages are listed below, but I will not discuss the immediate corrective actions, since they are quite involved. The stoppages we were trained in were 1. Rifle fails to fire; 2. Bolt does not lock; 3. Bolt locked, but rifle still does not fire; 4. Rifle fails to feed cartridge; 5. Rifle fails to extract a cartridge case.

It was emphasized that proper care and cleaning of one's rifle could drastically reduce the occurrence of stoppages. The reliability of the M-1 rifle was legendary in the Marine Corps, and most Marines were sorry to see it eventually replaced. It was emphasized that the rifle should be carefully cleaned as soon as possible after firing, and if it has not been fired for some time, it should be cleaned before firing. Also, if your ammunition gets wet or dirty, or if light corrosion forms on the cartridges, wipe it off at once.

We were also instructed to not forget to give the wooden parts of our rifle the same amount of care given to the metal parts. If the wood was allowed to dry out, it would crack or rot. This could be prevented by applying linseed oil to the wood. However, we were warned to take care not to get linseed oil on the metal parts of the rifle. Linseed oil on metal dries into a sticky film that is hard to remove. The way to apply the linseed oil was by placing a little in the palm of the hand and rubbing it into the wood until the wood is dry and shiny. Then wipe any excess linseed oil off the wood before reassembling the weapon. That completed the advanced and intensive instruction we received on the M-1 rifle at Camp Matthews.

As mentioned, mornings were in the classroom and afternoons on the firing range. As also mentioned, a vital part of training for record day was referred to as the "snapping-in period," which involved the recruit practicing in each of the firing positions until he found the most comfortable positioning of his body. Now, this might sound strange to the reader who would consider the posture of a firing position cut and dried. Not so! Although the title of the position remains the same, the nomenclature or posture of each individual's body can have numerous differences. For example, the posture of a 6 foot 180 pound heavy set recruit can be significantly different than a 5 foot, 7 inch, 130 pound slender recruit. For each recruit to achieve the highest score he was capable of obtaining on record day, it was important for him to find those individual postures for each firing position that provided both comfort and reduction of physical stress while firing. The positions at first seemed awkward and somewhat cumbersome but became routine by the time record day arrived. And all of us agreed that the time and effort required to master those positions was well spent and that "snapping in" was essential preparation to firing for record. The four positions for record firing of the M-1 are shown in the pictures at the end of the chapter as noted.

Before assuming each position, the loop sling of the rifle is adjusted high on the arm as shown in the illustration, tightened to the recruit's comfort level but tight enough to prevent any movement of the rifle while sighting in and firing. The firing positions and how to assume them are shown in the order used on record day. We were required to study these positions carefully and follow the instructions given.

1. <u>Standing position</u> shown in picture 18. The correct posture for this firing position was virtually the same for all recruits regardless of body shape or weight, unlike the kneeling, sitting, and prone positions. However, this position was the most difficult to keep the rifle perfectly still while aiming and firing. Therefore, it was essential to have the rifle sling cinched tight on the upper arm.

2. <u>The Kneeling position</u> is shown in picture 19, the <u>Sitting position</u> in picture 20, and the <u>Prone position</u> in picture 21. Additional pictures of recruits during snapping in training are shown in pictures 22, 23, 24, and 25. Notice the kneeling, sitting, and prone positions. The importance of sling adjustment is shown and demonstrated by the instructor in pictures 26, 27, and 28.

Finally, the day we were waiting for arrived - Record Day. We were on the range at sunrise, and it was going to be a long day. Nerves were tense, stress was peaked, and hopes were high. Hope for that coveted Rifle Expert badge, but if not, the Rifle Sharpshooters badge was great. And if expert and sharpshooter were not attained, the Rifle Marksman badge would be quite acceptable. Anything to avoid the stigma of not qualifying.

We would fire 50 rounds, 10 from the standing position, 10 from the kneeling position, 10 from the sitting position, and 20 from the prone position. Each round was worth 5 points if it were a bullseye, which would give a maximum score of 250. Pictures 29, 30, and 31 show recruits checking the official scoreboard for their score after completing firing in one of the positions. The trick was to get to a 190 score as soon as possible, thus assuring qualification as marksman; then bear down hard on achieving 210 for sharpshooter and finally 220 for expert.

Pictures 32, 33, and 34 show members of the platoon waiting for their turn on the firing line. In the bottom picture, the second recruit from the right is our American Indian Pvt. Patrick. Picture 35 shows our two Drill Instructors, SDI Beeson on the end and JDI Chapman to his right, who monitored closely every recruit's progress.

Finally, my turn came. I adjusted the rifle's loop sling tightly around my arm to hold the rifle steady while aiming and firing to avoid any slight movement which could cause large errors when 200, 300, 500 yards away from the target. I assumed the standing position as taught and would fire ten rounds from that position. Before firing that first round, as before every round fired and after taking aim, I took a deep breath as instructed, let half of It out, then held it, while slowly squeezing, not pulling the trigger, until BAM, which came as a surprise because of that slow squeeze. After firing those ten rounds, I assumed the kneeling position for the next ten rounds, and after that, the sitting position for ten rounds.

Finally, I assumed the prone position, my favorite position, for the final 20 rounds. I fired 19 of those rounds, but before I could fire the 20th and last round, SDI Beeson called a halt to my firing. I didn't know why, and I didn't know what my score was, but I was pretty sure I had Sharpshooter in the bag. As it turned out, my score was 215, and if that last round I had yet to fire was a bullseye, my score would be 220 and I would qualify as Expert.

As I mentioned, SDI Beeson wanted me to fire expert. He called a halt to my firing to impress on me the importance of that last round and give me time to compose myself and calm down. He told me to relax, take all the time I wanted, that there was no hurry to fire that last round, and to ensure that everything felt right before I did. He even lit the smoking lamp so I could have a cigarette to help relax nerves. Like I mentioned, rifle qualification was a time when even the Drill Instructors became almost human, and this was one of those "almost human" moments for SDI Beeson.

Finally, it was time. I assumed the prone position, and with a quick prayer to heaven, sighted in, took that deep breath, let half of it out, held the sight steady on the bullseye, and squeezed that trigger ever so slowly until BAM. The round was on its way. I waited nervously until the scorer in the pit raised the pole with the marker. Finally, he did, and it showed that the round had gone through the top left portion of the bullseye. The Expert badge was mine. The Drill Instructors congratulated me, along with some of my fellow recruits. There were some others who qualified as Expert, but not many. Many qualified as Sharpshooters, but I believe the majority qualified as Marksman. And yes, we had a few who didn't qualify and had to suffer the stigma of that for a short time, marching in back of the platoon shouting insults to themselves to advertise the fact that they had not qualified.

The major activity of boot camp, rifle qualification, was over and we were about to leave Camp Matthews and return to the Recruit Depot. But before we did, we had to fire the .45 caliber pistol, the standard military sidearm, for qualification. Pictures 36 and 37 show illustrations of the .45 caliber pistol's nomenclature.

The muzzle velocity of the weapon was 802 feet per second, and the .45 caliber round so big that the joke was, if you hit a person in the finger, you would knock them to the ground in shock. The maximum effective range was 25 yards, but the recoil of the weapon made it difficult to fire it accurately. Another story going around was that if you could hit a barn door with a round from this weapon, you were an average marksman with the .45 caliber pistol. Picture 38, which shows the size of the barrel, gives an indication of the size of the round and the recoil involved, giving credence to both stories. I qualified with the weapon, but barely.

We also got to disassemble, reassemble, and fire the .30 caliber Browning Automatic Rifle (BAR), but we didn't have to qualify in it. A picture of the weapon and its basic nomenclature are shown in picture 39. This was an outstanding weapon with great firepower, and we all really enjoyed firing it. It was an air-cooled, gas-operated, magazine-fed, shoulder weapon with bipod. Some general facts about the BAR: Weight - 19.4 pounds; magazine capacity - 20 rounds; maximum effective range - 500 yards; Rates of fire (Rounds per minute) - Normal cyclic rate - 550; Slow cyclic rate - 350.

In the Marines, at the time, each fire team was built around a BAR. This gave each rifle squad three of these weapons and each rifle platoon nine of them. Because of its great fire power, it was the most vital weapon of the platoon. All members of the platoon, whether they were armed with the BAR or not, had to know all about it so that any of them could man the weapon if the BAR man was killed or wounded. Any member of the unit could become the BAR man replacement since BAR carriers were primary targets of the enemy.

Due to the heavy weight of the BAR, it was a standard joke that the smallest men in the platoon were assigned as BAR men. As I said, we recruits didn't have to qualify on the BAR, but we all thoroughly enjoyed firing it. Pictures 40, 41, and 42 show recruits assembling the BAR until the watchful eye of an instructor. When firing the BAR, you had to grip it really tight because if you didn't, with the rate of fire and the recoil it had, it would be pointing straight up after a few rounds had fired.

We also were able to fire the .30 caliber Browning Heavy Machine Gun for familiarization only. This machine gun was used in World War I, World War II, the Korean War, and later in the Vietnam War, which should leave no doubt about how good a weapon it was. It was a tripod mounted, recoil operated, belt fed, water-cooled weapon with a rate of fire of 400-600 rounds per minute and a range of 1000 meters. It was called a heavy machine gun for a reason - it was heavy, yet this gave it great stability and reliability and made it an outstanding defense weapon. Picture 43 shows the machine gun and its two-man crew. Pulling the trigger on this weapon and watching the torrent of lead utterly devastate a target was, to put it mildly, a rush for all of us.

Qualifying with the M-1 rifle, firing the Browning Automatic Rifle and the .30 caliber Browning Heavy Machine Gun were the highlights of our three weeks at Camp Matthews. Before I leave the subject of Camp Matthews, I want to mention two other events that occurred while we were there. The first event involved a steep, high hill that was located near our barracks area. If I remember correctly, this steep hill was referred to as "Old Baldy."

Our acquaintance with "Old Baldy" came about as a result of our again stirring up the wrath of the Drill Instructors over something we had failed to do or had not done up to their standards. Or perhaps we hadn't done anything to deserve what was coming. Perhaps it was something all the Drill Instructors did with their recruits before leaving Camp Matthews in order to reestablish iron discipline after easing up just a tiny bit during qualification, and to remind us that we were still maggots and the Drill Instructors had total control. Whatever the cause, we were about to suffer the consequences.

We were ordered to pack up our duffel bags to the full with all our clothing and other items and to form up outside in formation. With our duffel bag packed full, it weighed around forty pounds. We formed up, were ordered to put our duffel bags on our shoulders and were then marched to the base of "Old Baldy." We were then ordered to lower ourselves to the squat position, which was painful to the legs with that 40-pound duffel bag on our shoulder. But the worst was yet to come.

We were ordered to "duckwalk" in cadence up steep "Old Baldy." Picture 44 shows the loaded duffel bag we had on our shoulders and picture 45 shows the position designated as "duckwalk." The exercise is called "duckwalk" because to walk while squatting you have to waddle like a duck to keep your balance. The Marines in the picture are carrying their rifles and are duckwalking on level ground. Even at that it is a grueling exercise. Now imagine that instead of that 9.5 pound rifle, you have a 40 pound duffel bag on your shoulder. Further imagine that instead of level ground, you are having to duckwalk up a fairly steep hill. That is pure agony.

It wasn't long before the platoon was totally bedraggled with us recruits falling out of line and cadence, dropping our duffel bags and falling to our knees to relieve the pain in our legs, with the Drill Instructors screaming and cursing at us, ordering us to place our duffel bags back on our shoulders, get back to the duckwalk position, and continue climbing "Old Baldy." This continued for some time, until finally it became obvious that there was nothing to be gained from further punishment. We recruits, some of us sobbing, some crying, some puking, were at the end of our endurance, and so the Drill Instructors called a halt and released us back to the barracks.

I don't think anyone made it to the top of "Old Baldy." Furthermore, I don't think the instructors expected anyone to do so. However, I will say this. Many of us, if not most of us, got further than we thought we would. And that was due to the sheer extra effort the Drill Instructors forced from us, and which we didn't know we had in us. Again, thinking back on it, it's clear that throughout boot camp the Drill Instructors used our fear of them to stir up an anger in us that would bring forth that extra effort to show those #@!&%* Drill Instructors just what we so-called maggots could do. To me, of all the physical demands and endurance tests we experienced in boot camp, this was the most painful.

The other event that occurred prior to our leaving Camp Matthews concerned one of our platoon members who was consistently screwing up and causing punishment to the whole platoon. One of our drill instructors - I forget whether it was SDI Beeson or JDI Chapman - called me aside as Right Guide, and reminded me that in a military organization, each member is responsible to the organization. When one member succeeds, all join in the success, and when one member screws up, all share in the punishment and responsibility to resolve the problem. As Right Guide of the platoon, the responsibility to handle the situation was primarily mine and the rest of the platoon members.

He suggested that I pick four or five other recruits, arrange a meeting with the offending recruit in a private area outside, and inform him that he either get squared away and stop bringing punishment on the platoon because of his failure to comply with the rules of behavior and discipline or bad things would be happening to him. The Drill Instructor made it clear that we were to deliver the message in a forceful manner.

Which we did. But only in a rough housing manner with pushing and shoving. No beating, no punches, hits, or strikes to the face or body, which was most fortunate for us. Because the recruit demanded and received his right to lodge a complaint with higher authority. The Battalion Executive Officer, a Major, convened a hearing at which I and the four or five other recruits who had joined me, were summoned to appear. We all totally refuted the recruit's claim that we had ganged up on him and given him a severe beating and emphasized that the only bodily contact had been a bit of pushing and shoving. Since there was no physical evidence of a beating or severe treatment, the matter was closed, and I and the other recruits were dismissed.

Soon after that, the offending recruit was gone, and we never saw him again. I suspect that, in view of his record of disciplinary problems, he was given a General or Bad Conduct discharge, and separated from the Corps on the grounds of failing to meet Marine Corps standards, which was probably the objective of his rebellious behavior all along.

Now fast forward to 1992 and the movie "A Few Good Men." The movie, starring Jack Nicholson, Tom Cruise, and Demi Moore, centered on the trial of two Marine enlisted men who had been ordered by their superior to conduct a midnight physical attack on another enlisted Marine in the unit who had been consistently screwing up, with the threat of more to come if he didn't change his behavior. Apparently the Marine attacked had a heart problem and died as a result of the physical punishment he had received. The two Marine attackers were charged with murder and brought to General Court Martial.

One of the central questions to be resolved at the court martial was who ordered the attack. Was it the two Marines' immediate superior, or was the attack ordered by higher command authority? That person would be charged with murder along with the two attackers. Apparently such attacks and threats, although in violation of the Uniform Code of Military Justice, were somewhat commonplace at the time in order to square away miscreants and disciplinary problems in a unit. They even had a name for such an event, a "Code Red."

Well, in the movie, the person who had ordered the attack by the two Marines on their fellow Marine was the Commanding Officer of the base. He was arrested, charged, and brought to Court Martial. As I was watching all this transpire on the screen, I had a feeling that it was all familiar to me. Then the light came on and I realized that the Code Red action in the movie of those two Marines against that Marine causing problems in their platoon was precisely what I and my fellow recruits in boot camp at Camp Matthews were instructed to do to the recruit causing problems in our platoon. The term Code Red was not in use back in 1956, and I suspect it was probably a term contrived by the movie's script writers. Nevertheless, the actions associated with it were the same, although in our case the person we were trying to square away was not seriously injured or harmed. But it was somewhat of a surreal experience, having a drama I was watching on the movie screen in 1992 take me back to a similar real-life drama I had experienced in 1956.

Camp Matthews had been the highlight of boot camp thus far, but our time there was concluded, and we boarded the buses for the trip back to the Recruit Training Depot in San Diego. With only a few weeks to go to graduation, the light at the end of that 12 week tunnel of boot camp was visible. We all were hoping that those weeks to be yet endured would go by quickly. How naive of us! By now we should have learned that in Marine Corps boot camp, the weeks, days, and hours do not go by quickly.

1

2

3

4

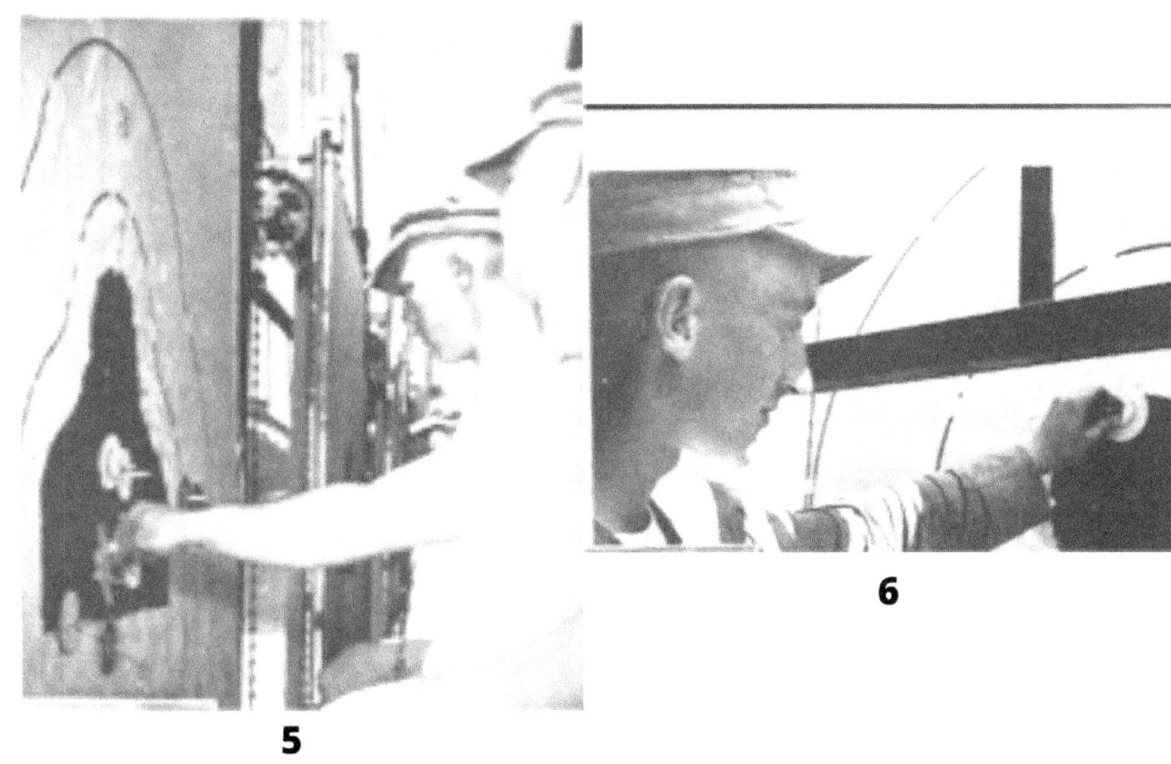

5

6

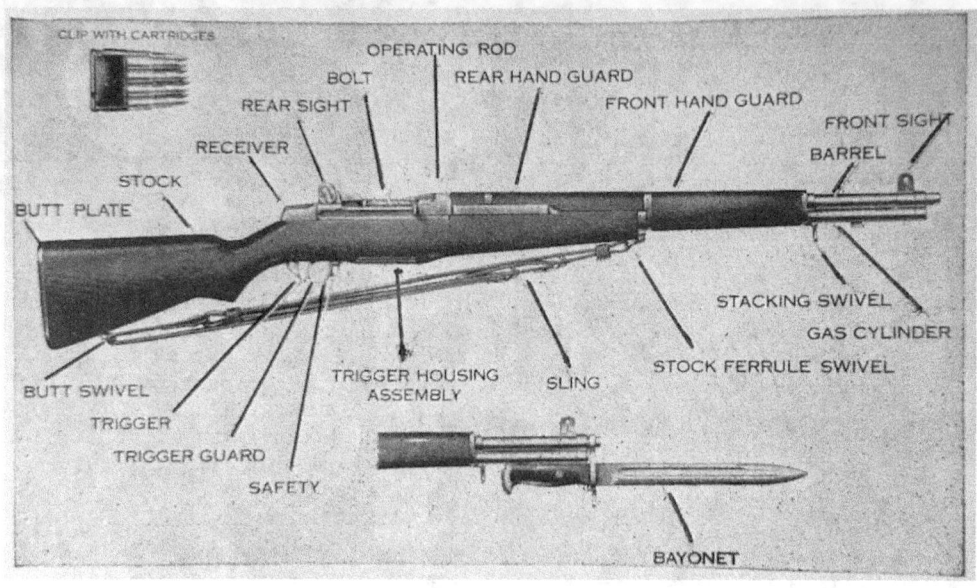

7 - Basic nomenclature of the M1 Rifle.

8 - The three main groups.

9   M-1 Trigger Housing Group

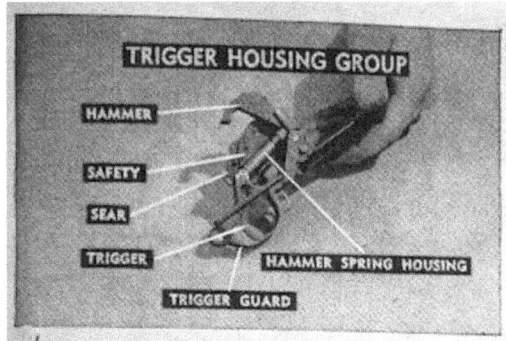

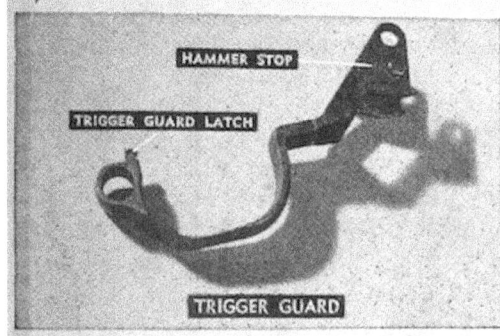
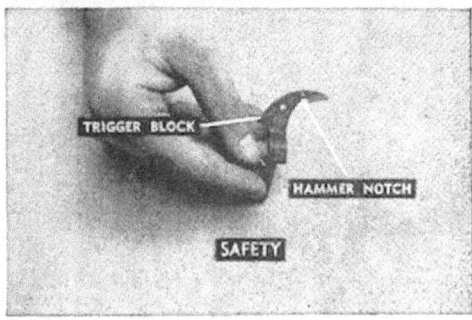
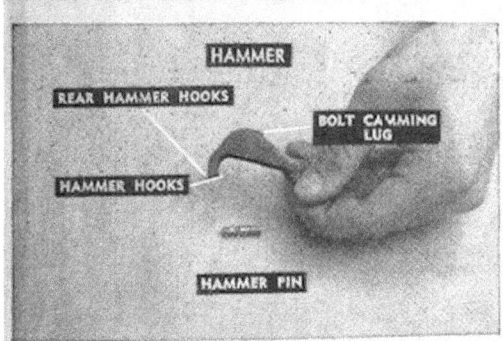
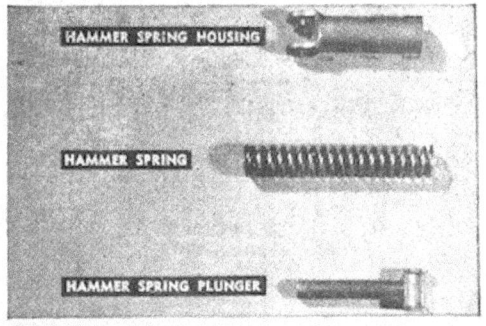
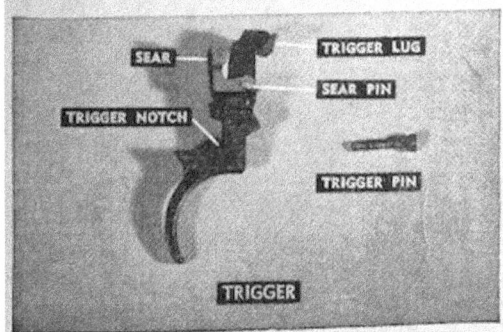
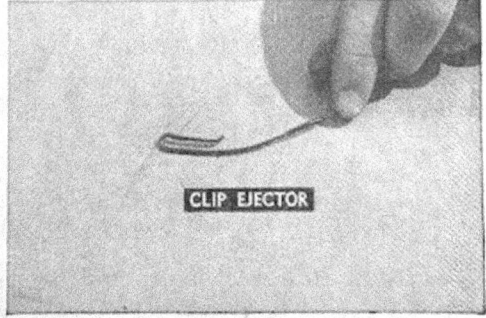

10   Barrel and Receiver Group

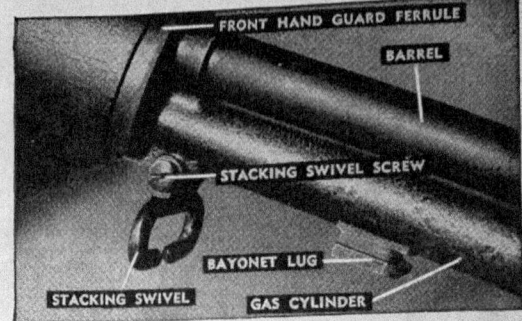
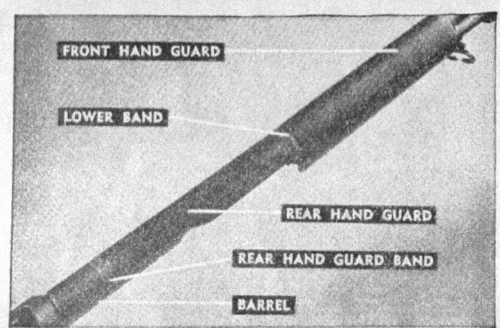

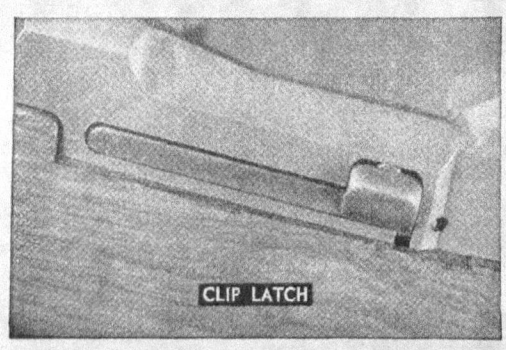

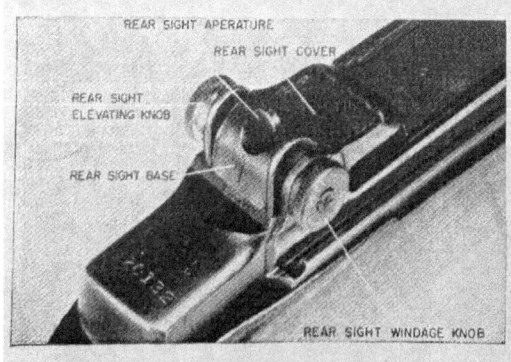
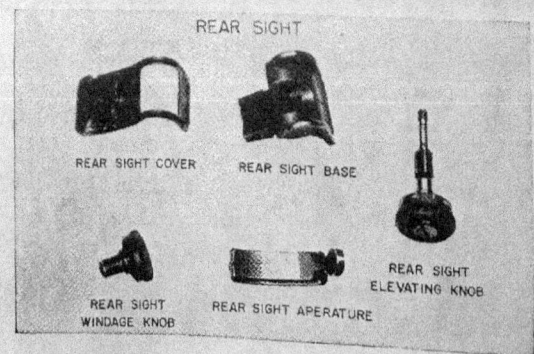

11 Barrel and Receiver Group (cont'd)

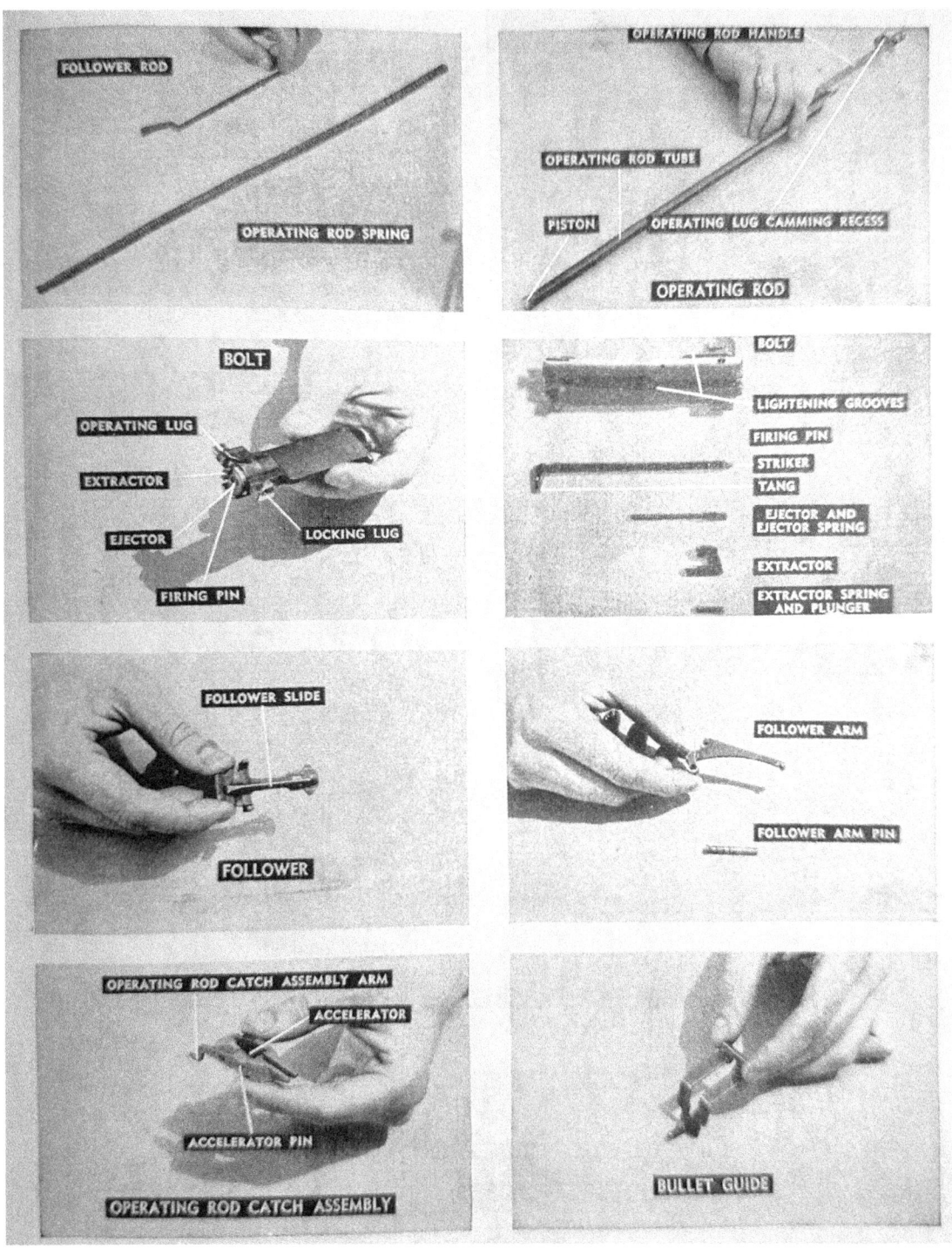

12 The Stock Group

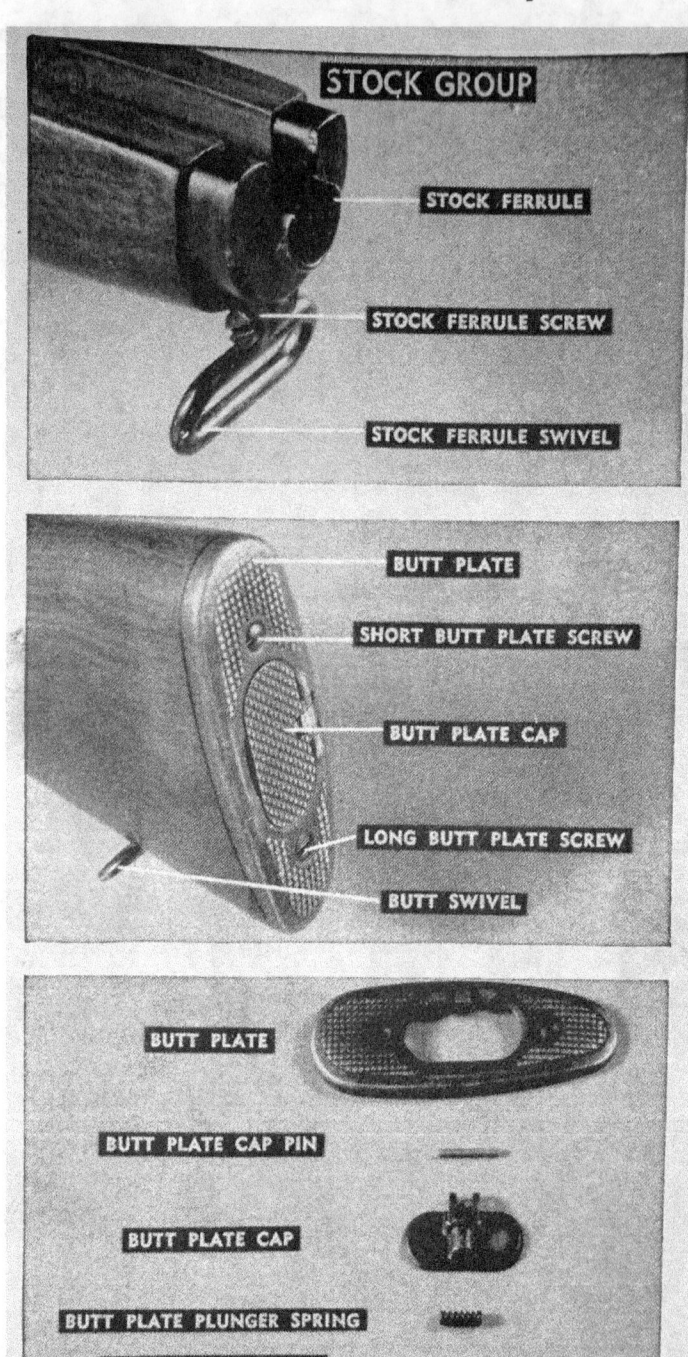

Ignition

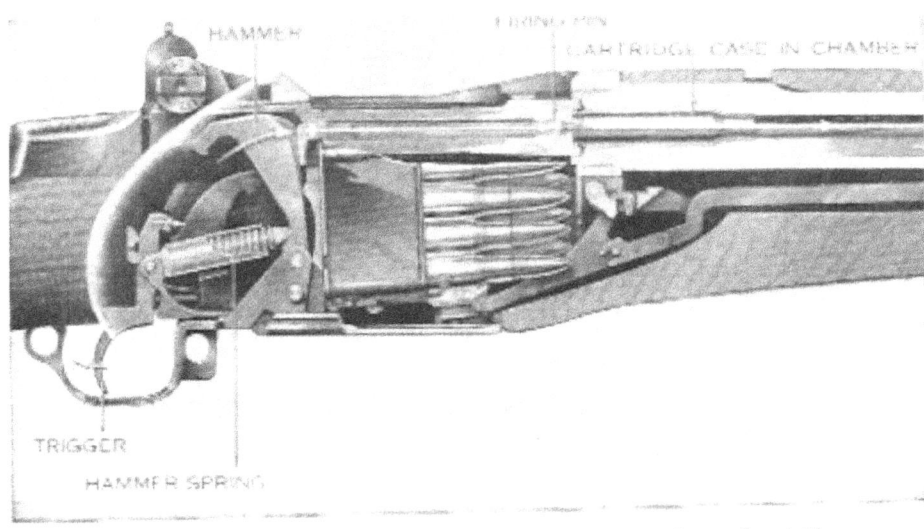

The hammer strikes firing pin and ignites primer at base of cartridge.

13

Action of the Gas

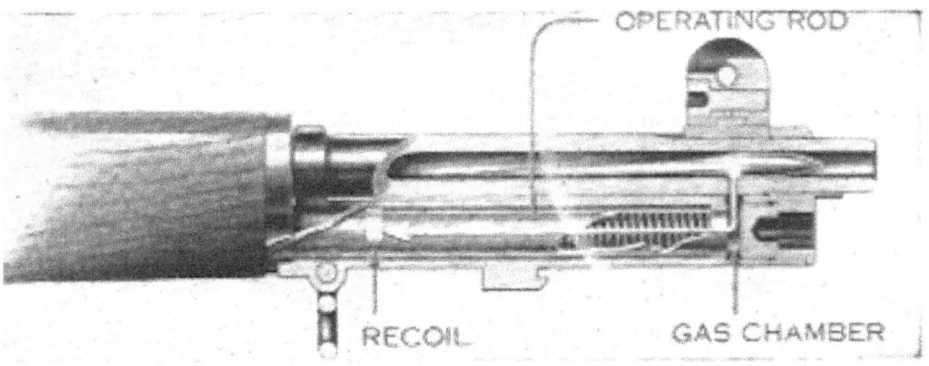

Gas strikes piston and drives operating rod to the rear.

14

Movement of the Operating Rod

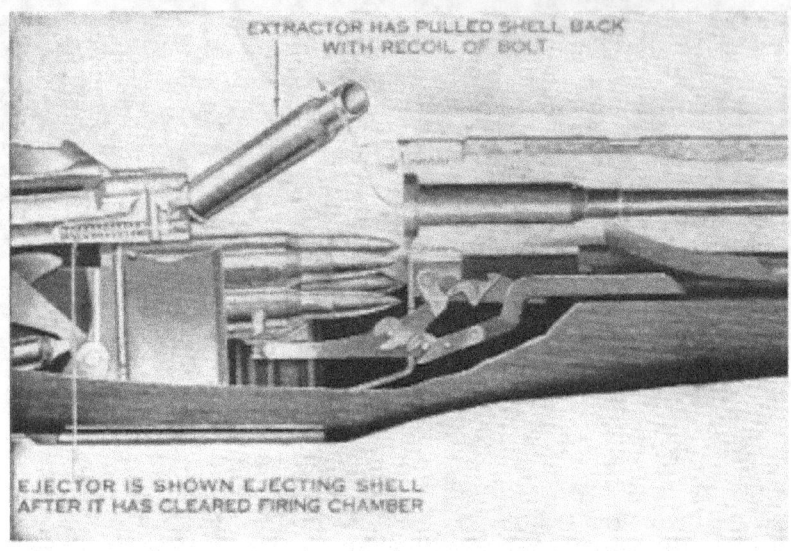

The ejector throws the empty cartridge out to the right.

15

Cocking of the Hammer

Bolt rides over hammer, forcing hammer back and thus cocking it.

16

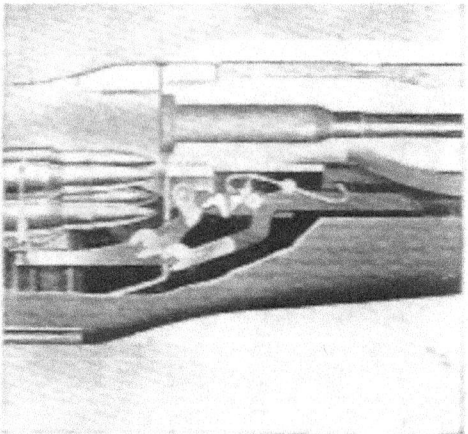

Follower, actuated by follower arm and rod, forces cartridge up in clip.

17

THE STANDING POSITION

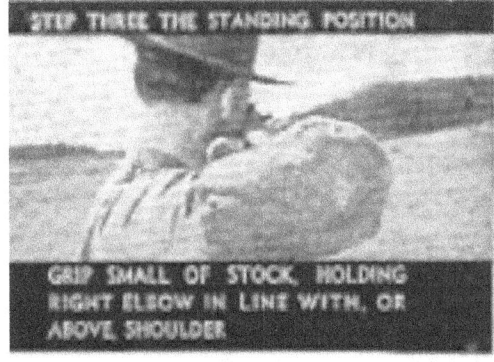

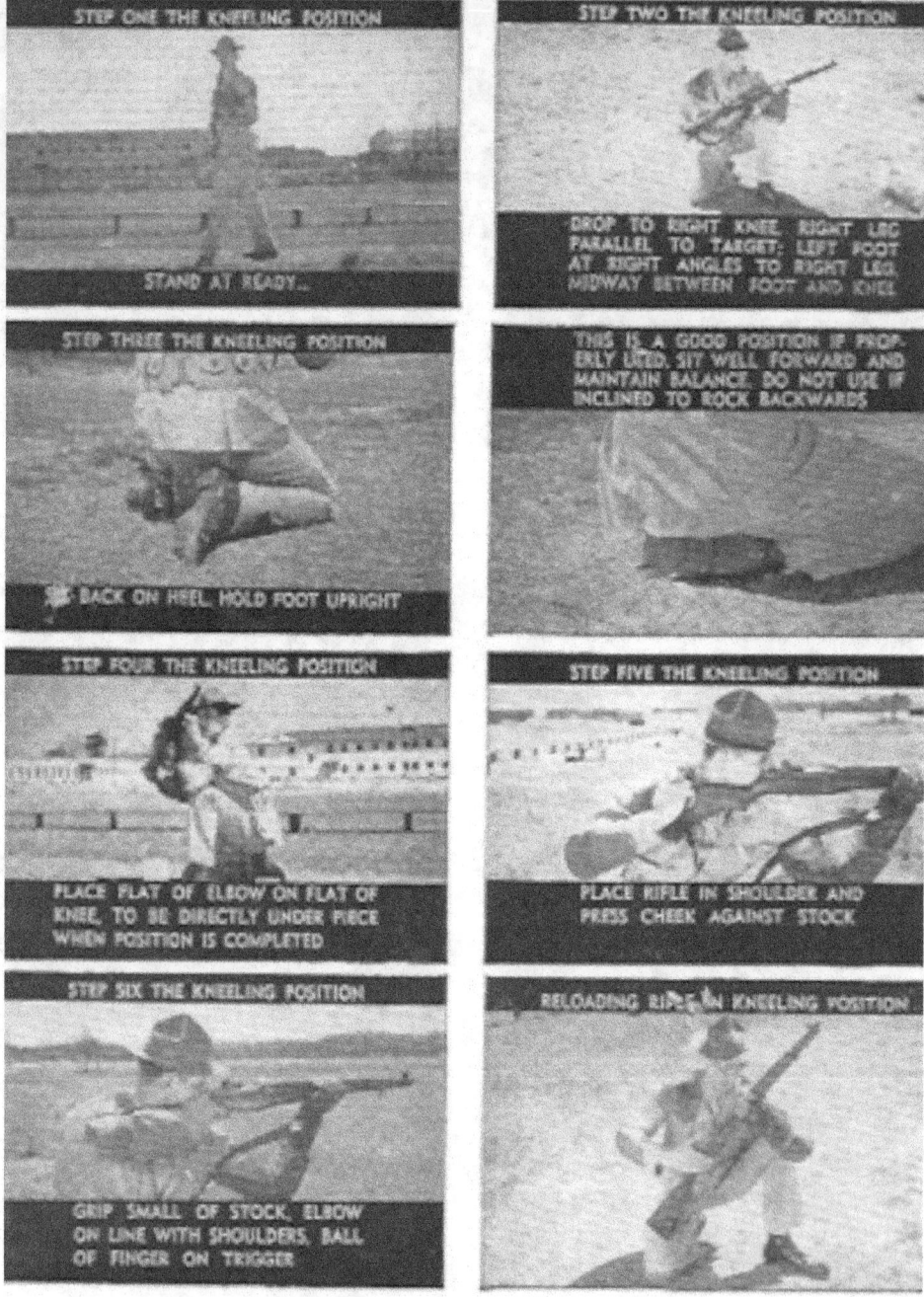

THE SITTING POSITION

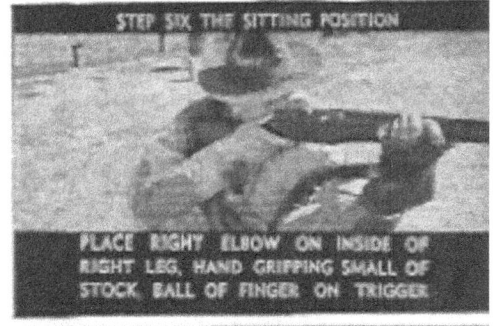

20

THE PRONE POSITION

22

23

24

25

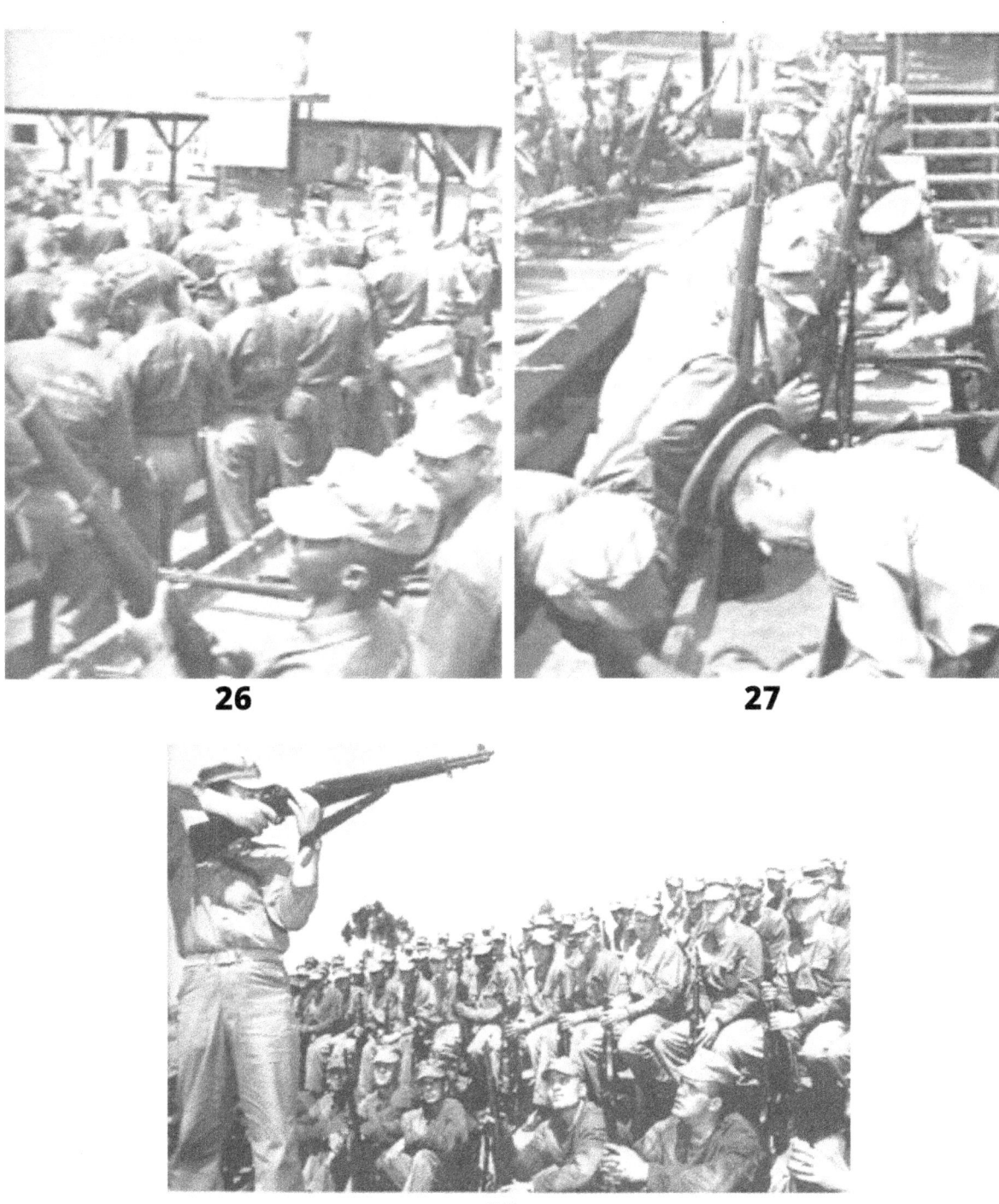

26

27

28

29

30 **31**

32

33

34

35

36

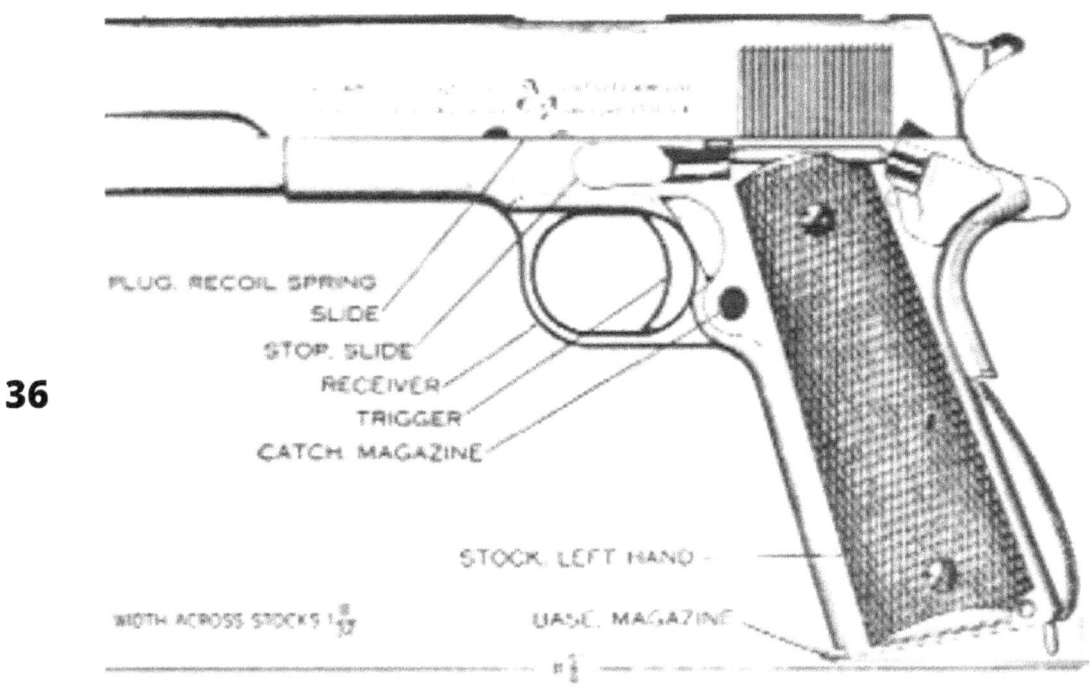

12.1 Basic Nomenclature (Mechanism in Forward Position).

37

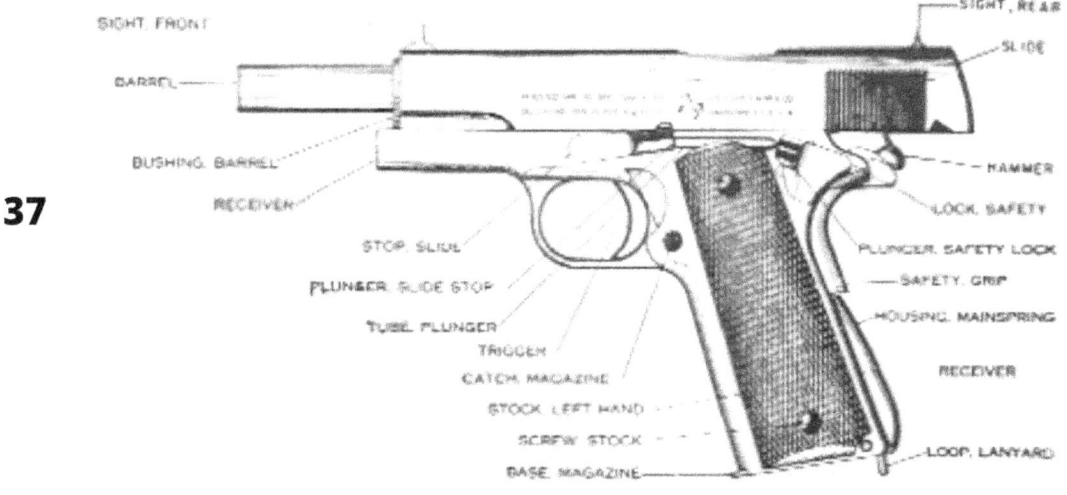

Basic Nomenclature (Mechanism in Recoil Position).

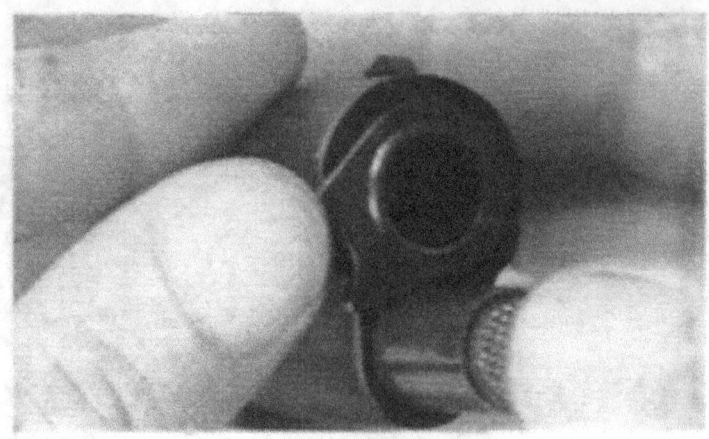

38

THE AUTOMATIC RIFLE

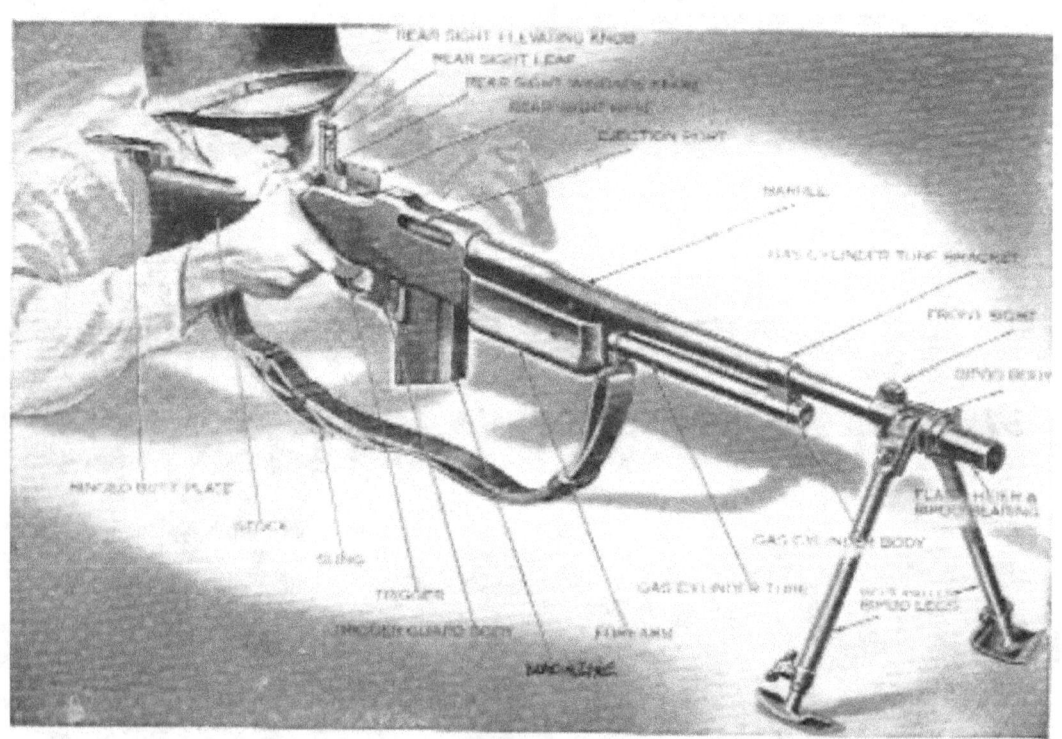

39

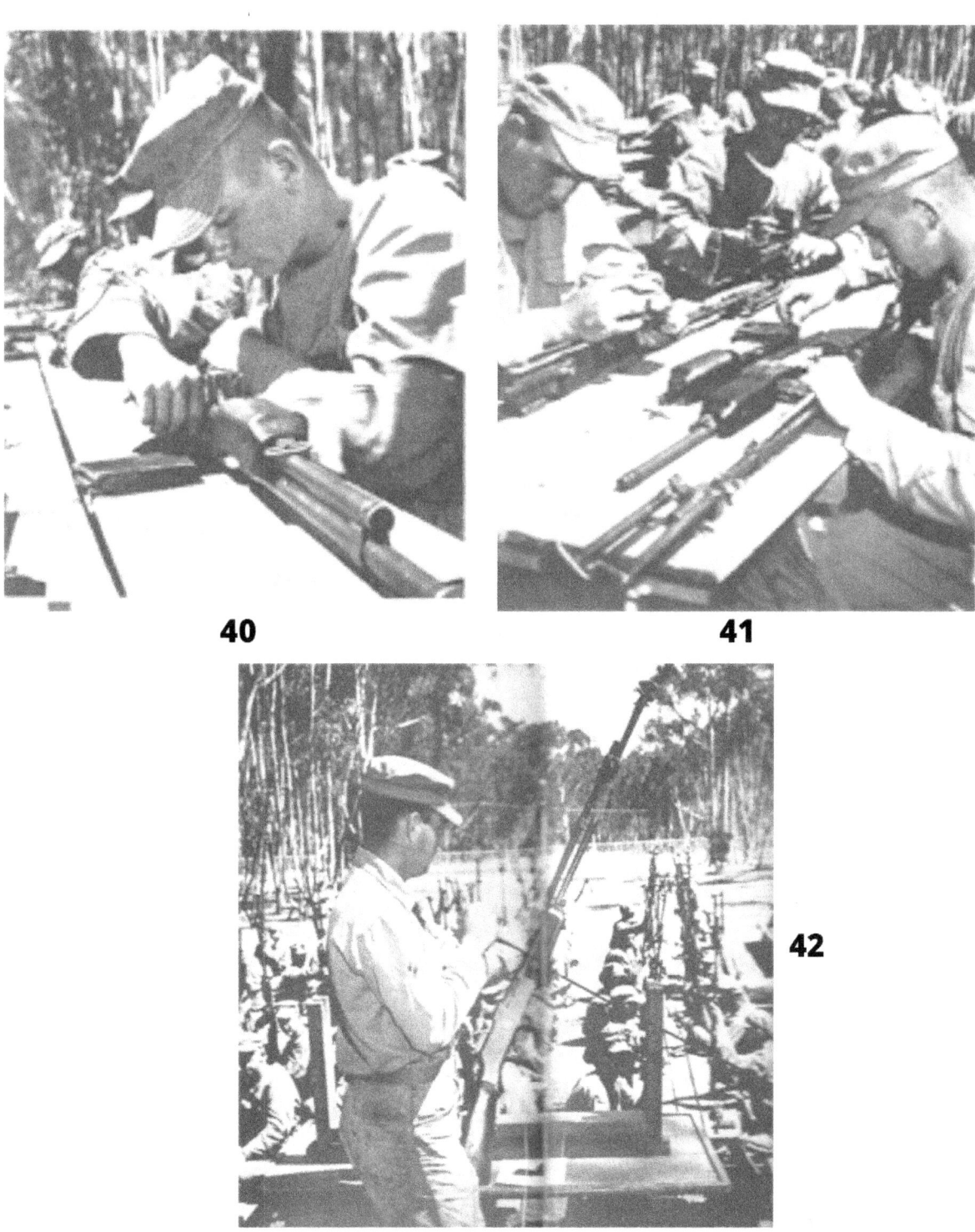

40

41

42

43

44

45

Chapter 16
Water Survival

Since the United States Marine Corps' primary mission is amphibious warfare, it is obvious that Marines need to know how to survive in water. Therefore, it stands to reason that boot camp would have a course of instruction on water training and survival. Granted, the Army also performed extensive and immensely successful amphibious warfare operations, the Normandy D-Day landings being the prime example. Nevertheless, amphibious warfare has been the bread and butter of the Marine Corps since the Revolutionary War.

In World War II, the dominant theater of operations for the Marines was the Pacific Theater. Marine Corps combat operations in World War II were almost exclusively centered in the Pacific, involving a vast domain of islands stretching towards Japan. To get close enough to Japan for allied Air Forces to have the range to conduct a strategic bombing campaign against the enemy's homeland, and eventually conduct an invasion of Japan if necessary, required an island hopping strategy, and this strategy necessarily centered on amphibious warfare.

Immediately following the Pearl Harbor attack, Japan had conducted extensive offensive operations throughout the Pacific region as far as Singapore and Burma, conquering these areas along with those strategic islands involved in an allied forces island hopping strategy towards Japan. Japan's army manned those islands and built up heavy defenses to repel any attempt of allied invasion. As I mentioned, the Army also conducted amphibious operations in the Pacific, but not to the extent of the Marines.

And so, the advance of the Allied forces in the Pacific was, to a great extent, due to the Marines' amphibious warfare and the brutal, no-holds barred, total war slugfest between the Marines and the fanatical Japanese in the bloody battles for these islands whose names resound in the annals of Marine Corps history, tradition, and heritage - Guadalcanal, Tarawa, Saipan, Iwo Jima, Okinawa - and others. The human cost to the Japanese in defending these islands was hundreds of thousands; the human cost to the Marine Corps in taking these islands was seventy-five thousand.

Back to our water training and survival classes in boot camp. It was inevitable that with the number of recruits in the platoon, there were some who didn't know how to swim. And to say that they were scared during this phase of training would be a gross understatement. Every recruit had to qualify in this basic Combat Water Survival Training Course, thus performing every exercise involved in the training, including going into the deep end of the pool with combat pack on the shoulders, regardless of whether or not they knew how to swim.

To successfully pass this water survival course, we had to swim a specific distance, tread water for a specific time, simulate rescuing a fellow Marine loaded down with combat equipment who was drowning in the surf, and other exercises as mentioned. The pictures shown at the end of the chapter depict some of these activities.

The Marine Corps will teach you how to swim, but anyone thinking about joining the Marines who doesn't know how to swim would be well-advised to take civilian swimming lessons before leaving for boot camp. The Marines' method for teaching recruits how to swim was somewhat antiquated and could be best described as "sink or swim." Picture 1 shows an instructor describing the steps involved in swimming to a group of recruits. The instruction basically went like this: "Reach out with one arm, grab the water and pull it back towards you; then reach out with the other arm, grab the water and pull it back towards you. Keep doing this, and while you are doing it, kick your feet up and down. Any questions?"

Treading water was obviously another important test recruits had to master. As I remember, four minutes was the time required for treading water without touching or holding on to the edge of the pool. Picture 2 shows an instructor at the side of the pool with a long pole. That long pole was used by the instructor to shove recruits who were learning to swim or who were treading water and trying to grab the edge of the pool back into the deep water. It was also used to pull recruits who had gone down for the third time back to the surface. The instructors closely monitored each student's progress and there were occasions when an instructor would dive in and rescue a recruit who had gone under and taking too much time to resurface.

That long pole provided great incentive to the recruit to make every effort to learn how to swim and tread water quickly.

We also had to leap into the water from a high distance to simulate abandoning ship. The high diving board shown in picture 3 was used for this purpose. Although the distance from the diving board to the water was woefully short of the distance from the deck of a troopship to the ocean below, it nevertheless had to suffice for the simulation. Add to that long distance from deck to ocean the rolling of the ship in high seas and the common occurrence of Marines getting seasick, and one can appreciate just how scary that long leap could be. The recruits who didn't know how to swim and who were afraid of the deep water were terrified over the prospect of jumping off that high board, but they had no choice. One way or the other, voluntarily or involuntarily, they were going to take the leap.

Picture 4 shows the instructor demonstrating to the recruits why cupping their face and facial features with the palm of the hand was important. This was to protect their face from injury if their long fall from the deck of a troopship ended with their hitting the water face down. Even though one could leap from the deck with feet downward and body straight, the trajectory of the body during that long fall could change. Therefore, eyes and facial features had to be protected.

Even good swimmers can struggle and panic when finding themselves in the water fully clothed and loaded down with their combat pack and equipment that was pulling them under. Therefore, water survival training included getting into the deep end of the pool with all combat gear and being able to shed that gear quickly – within ten seconds if I remember correctly. As I mentioned before, during amphibious landings, it was the objective of the Navy landing craft operator, not to mention the hope of the Marines aboard his craft, that he would judge the waves correctly so he could ride a wave to get them as close to the beach as possible, ideally so they could step out in ankle deep water or even on sand. However, this was not always the case, and it was common to step out of the landing craft into knee deep, waist deep, or even shoulder deep water. Thus, the danger of being swept off one's feet by the tide and sinking under the weight of one's combat gear and drowning in the surf was very real, and the ability to shed that gear quickly was a life and death matter.

This training is shown in picture 5 of the instructor with the combat pack lecturing the recruits. Another requirement was for the recruit, after shedding that combat pack and preventing it from pulling him under, was not to lose it, but to take advantage of the buoyancy of the combat pack and swim from one side of the pool to the other while holding on to it and bringing it with him.

The instructors worked to train those recruits who were afraid of the deep water to submerge themselves without panicking. They would do this by degrees, starting with short periods of submersion, and when the recruit could master this, increase the length of submersion gradually until the recruit, if not rid of his fear of deep water, could at least overcome it for an acceptable length of time.

An important lesson the instructors emphasized was the natural buoyancy of the human body and its capability to float with minimal effort in treading water. To panic and thrash about in the water reduced this buoyancy and capability to float and was therefore fatal. The bottom line was that it was mandatory for the Marine who feared deep water to reduce that fear to where it was manageable and gain enough self-confidence to enable him to perform the three essentials - relax, breathe, and survive.

Finally, we were advised to always try to revive a person who seems to have drowned, and we were given instruction on artificial respiration as follows.

1. First Step: Kneel facing the patient's head and place your hands on the patient's back. Your thumbs should just touch, and the heels of your hands should be just below a line running between the armpits. This position is shown in picture 6.
2. Second Step: With the compression stage, rock slowly forward until your arms are approximately vertical. This allows the weight of the upper part of your body to exert slow even pressure downward and push the air out of the patient's lungs. This second step of compression is shown in picture 7.
3. Third Step: The next step is the lung-filling stage when you release the downward pressure and rock back slowly, sliding your hands to the patient's arms just above the elbows. Continue to rock backward and raise the arms until resistance and tension are felt at the patient's shoulders. This lung-filling stage is shown in picture 8.
4. Fourth Step: The fourth and final step is to gently lower the arms of the patient to the ground which completes the cycle. The fourth step is shown in picture 9.

Repeat the full cycle 10 to 12 times a minute. If possible, take turns with another person in repeating the cycle but do not break the rhythm of the cycle. Wrap the patient in a blanket and when he is conscious, give him a warm drink such as coffee or tea.

And with that, we concluded water survival and moved on to another delightful experience of boot camp - the gas chamber.

> *"Demonstrate to the world that there is no better friend, and no worse enemy than a United States Marine."*
>
> — Gen. James "Chaos" Mattis

1

2

3

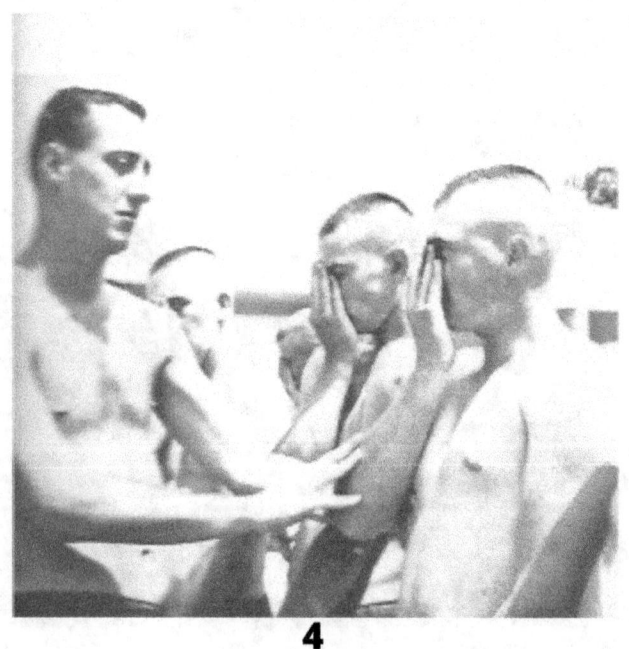

4

5

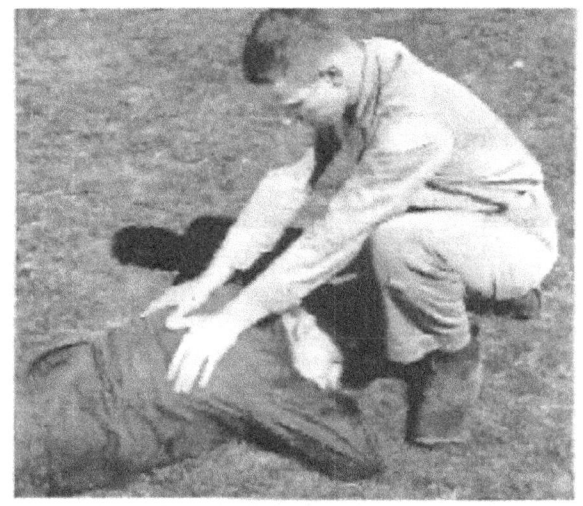

First step.
6

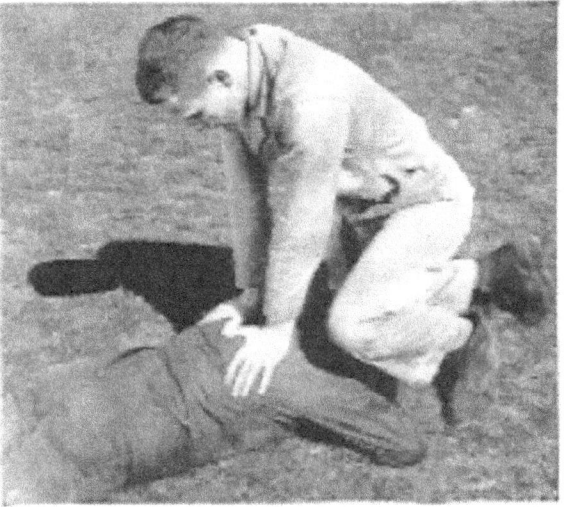

Second step.
7

Third step.

8

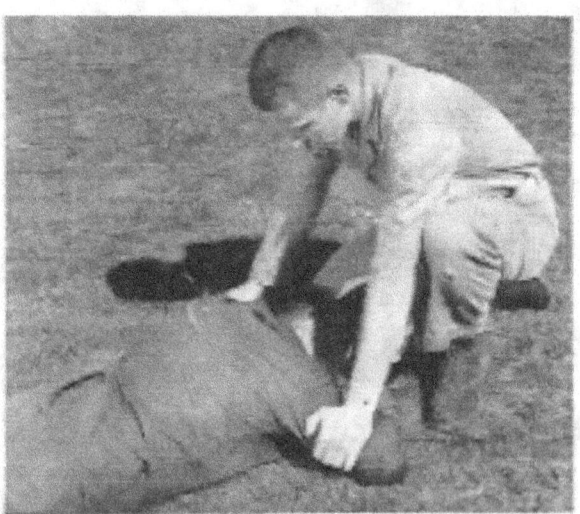

Fourth step.

9

Chapter 17
Gas Chamber

After the fun of water survival, we were scheduled for another delightful challenge - that of the gas chamber. The enemy could use poison gas at any time, so being prepared for it, knowing how to recognize it when it comes, and knowing how to use the protective equipment issued to each Marine was mandatory.

The National World War I Museum and Memorial in Kansas City, Missouri contains the history of the first usage of poison gas as part of its military history collection from which the following is taken. On April 22, 1915, a wave of asphyxiating gas was released from cylinders embedded in the ground by German specialists. This gas covered the Allied line, causing panic and a struggle to survive a new type of weapon. The attack forced two colonial French divisions from their positions, creating a five-mile gap in the Allied line defending the city of Ypres. This was the first effective use of poison gas on the Western front, and the debut of Germany's newest weapon in its chemical arsenal - chlorine gas, which irritated the lung tissue causing a choking effect that could cause death.

A British officer described the effect of the gas on the French colonial soldiers: "A panic-stricken rabble with gray faces and protruding eyeballs, clutching their throats and choking as they ran, many of them dropping in their tracks and lying on the sodden earth with limbs convulsed and features distorted in death."

After this initial use of poison gas, the technology and operational tactics of chemical gas warfare quickly developed and were implemented by the Germans and the Allies throughout the war, including various gases and liquids, practical gas masks, and gas alarm equipment. Combatant nations established chemical warfare units and schools to train them in the tactics of offensive and defensive gas warfare.

By the end of the war, the Germans produced the most poison gas, with 68,000 tons, the French second with approximately 36,000 tons, and the British produced approximately 25,000 tons. About three percent of gas casualties were fatal, but hundreds of thousands suffered temporary or permanent injuries.

Getting back to our training in gas warfare during boot camp, there was an entire chapter on the subject in our personal guidebook for Marines. Classroom instruction was topped off with a visit to the gas chamber. We learned that all gases used in warfare are categorized in two classes - the Persistent Class or the Non-Persistent Class. A persistent gas is one used primarily to disable personnel and to delay or restrict their use of terrain and material. This type of gas would be effective from 10 minutes to 12 hours. A non-persistent gas is one used in high concentrations to kill or disable personnel before any preventive action can be taken by them. This type of gas would be effective for less than 10 minutes.

The use of chemical agents in warfare can be used in one or a combination of the following ways:

1. <u>Casualty Attacks</u>: This involves a surprise employment of chemical gases to produce a maximum number of casualties to personnel. The desired effects would be achieved through the release of high concentrations of the gas in a short period of time as referred to above. Surprise must be achieved in this attack because well-trained opposing troops, through the proper use of their gas masks and other protective equipment would neutralize the desired effects. Either a persistent or non-persistent gas could be used in this attack, but usually a non-persistent gas would be used.

2. <u>Harassing Attacks</u>: This is a chemical attack that would force opposing troops to wear their gas masks and other protective equipment for long periods of time. A gas would be used that would prolong the decontamination process and add to the discomfort and irritation of the troops under attack. Therefore, it is more likely that a persistent gas would be used in this attack rather than a non-persistent gas.

3. <u>Neutralization Attacks</u>: This type of attack is designed to enable troops to move in and occupy the area neutralized. However, the troops occupying the area would be taking a calculated risk since persistent gas would be used to neutralize the area and the duration of the effectiveness of the gas would vary.

The effects of any chemical gas agent on the human body will vary. Some agents are obviously more harmful than others; however, sometimes the same chemical agent can be more harmful at one time than at another time. The direct effects of the agent are constant in nature, but the reaction of individuals to different chemical agents may vary in many cases. We were taught a variety of chemical gases and their effects on a person subjected to a concentration of such gases who is without protective equipment. These were as follows:

1. <u>Blister Gases</u>: This type of gas acts primarily on the eyes and skin, especially hot, moist skin such as the crotch and armpits. Also, when breathed, further damage will be sustained by the respiratory system. When absorbed, these gases may cause poisoning of the system. Arsenic is a property of some blister gases, and gases containing this substance are more dangerous than others. The harmful effects are usually delayed for several hours; however, pain may occur immediately in some cases.

2. <u>Choking Gases</u>: Choking gases, as the name implies, primarily irritate the breathing passages, especially the lungs. The damage may be delayed as much as one or two days, and the victim will suffer effects somewhat similar to those caused by pneumonia. In liquid form, the gas may cause burns to the eyes or a blistering of the skin.

3. <u>Blood and Nerve Gases</u>: In high concentrations, these chemical agents may act within a few seconds and after only a few breaths. These gases affect the nervous system and the blood stream. Lower concentrations of the gas are also dangerous, but sometimes the effects are delayed for several hours. They may cause an intense flow of tears and irritation to the nose and throat.

4. <u>Vomiting Gases</u>: These gases irritate the eyes, nose, and throat, and will cause headaches, vomiting, coughing, sneezing and considerable discomfort.

Concentrations of this gas in open field conditions is unlikely to cause permanent injury. Concentration in close areas, however, will be dangerous. After being subjected to this gas, and then applying the gas mask, may result in extreme discomfort; however, the gas mask should not be removed.

5. <u>Tear Gases</u>: Tear gases cause pain to the eyes and tears will flow freely. They may also sting the skin, especially the freshly shaved face, the neck, and any moist surface of the body. Tear gas was the chemical agent we were introduced to and became intimately familiar with in the gas chamber. We were also given an open field demonstration of tear gas as shown in picture 1 at the end of the chapter.

6. <u>Screening Smokes</u>: Screening smokes under open field conditions are usually harmless; however, liquid screening smokes may cause burns to skin and clothing. Screening smoke used by friendly forces does not necessarily require use of the gas mask. However, screening smoke used by an enemy may contain poisonous gas; therefore, apply the mask and test for gas. We were given a demonstration of screening smoke as shown in the previous illustration involving tear gas in picture 1.

The Marine's individual defense against chemical gases consists basically of two actions:

1. Put on your personal protective equipment. This may seem obvious, but it is common for individuals to delay responding to a warning of potential gas attack until the last moment because of the discomfort entailed wearing the equipment. This equipment will protect the eyes, nose, throat, lungs, and body. Above all, remember that the gas mask is the number one protection against a chemical agent attack. Other protective equipment referred to above that may be issued to each Marine to protect against chemical agents is a parka, trousers, socks, gloves, and shoe coverings. Eye-shields may also be issued to protect the eyes when the gas mask is not worn. These additional protective equipment items would be issued before particular operations or prior to an enemy's anticipated concentrated use of chemical agents.

2. The second action that can improve the Marine's individual defense against chemical attack is to change his position to an upwind location, or an area of higher elevation. The wind can move the gases away from him and the higher elevation can serve to reduce the concentration of gases. Also, if there is any kind of shelter nearby, make use of it to reduce exposure and afford some additional protection.

The field protective gas mask we were taught to use in 1956 was at the time the best of its kind that science had produced. Gas masks today are much more advanced, as well as more comfortable. Whenever the Marine uses his gas mask, he must always make sure that it fits, and that no air can enter, using the procedures he was taught. He must always remember that when the word "GAS" is given, he is to immediately stop breathing, and try not to take another breath, even if your breath has just been exhaled, until your mask is tightly adjusted. The ability to hold one's breath for 30 seconds or more should be developed. Pictures 2, 3, 4, and 5 show the instructors training recruits on the gas mask, how it works, how to put it on, how to service it, and how to care for it.

As I said, the gas masks we had in 1956 shown in the pictures, were state of the art at the time. Compared to what we have today, they appear downright ancient. You could carry your mask in several positions, using the position most favorable to the occasion and considering what other combat equipment you were carrying. These positions are side carry, leg carry, chest carry, and back carry, and are shown in pictures 6, 7, 8, 9, 10, and 11.

It was interesting to learn that various detection devices have been designed for both the detection and identification of war gases by a change of color. They are also used to indicate the completion of decontamination procedures. These detector kits are issued either as unit equipment or personnel equipment. Therefore, the presence of gas can be indicated without individuals having to depend upon their senses alone to detect gas. War gases smell different to different individuals, and some of the gases are odorless. Moreover, the many odors of battle might well mask any odor of poison gases. Therefore, the importance of being able to identify the gases by their color was emphasized to us.

A Marine may be called upon to perform any or all of the personal decontamination measures. He may be called on to act as a member of a decontamination team, in which case specially trained personnel would act as supervisors. Or, in emergencies, he may have to act alone. Therefore, the Marine had to be familiar with the following various decontamination agents and procedures for their use: 1. Bleach (chloride or lime); 2. Decontaminating Agent M4 (DANC); 3. Washing Soda (Sodium Carbonate); 4. Caustic Soda (Lye); 5. Water or Steam; 6. Fuels and Solvents; and 7. Protective Ointment.

The climax of the Gas Chamber course was, of course, the gas chamber itself. We all entered this room in a building with no windows and one door which was locked behind us. The room was then filled with tear gas. We were then ordered to take off our gas masks and sing the first verse of the Marine Corps hymn. We felt the full effects of the tear gas in the eyes, the throat, and on the skin, and wanted out of that room immediately. So naturally we started to sing faster and faster. The Drill Instructor ordered us to stop and begin again at the beginning of the verse and sing at the correct pace. So, we did, and finally the Drill Instructor opened the door and told us to exit the building. Pictures 12, 13, and 14 show the effects the tear gas had on us recruits and the relief on getting out of that building.

That phase of training ended with the warning to never, never remove your gas mask until you receive the word to do so and remember that some gases are odorless and colorless and the air around you must be tested with a detector kit to ensure that no gas remains around you. And with that, our training in chemical warfare during boot camp ended, to be continued periodically during our tour of duty. Now, we were to embark on a phase of training that we were all looking forward to - bayonet training.

"Marines I see as two breeds; Rottweilers and Dobermans, because Marines come in two varieties - big and mean, or skinny and mean. They're aggressive on the attack and tenacious on defense. They've got really short hair and they always go for the throat."

Rear Admiral "Jay" R. Stark

1

2

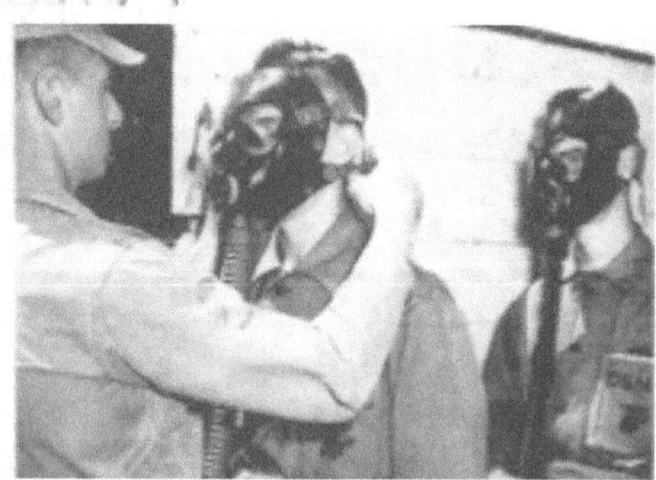

3

4

5

Side carry, first step.
6

Side carry, final step.
7

Carrier in chest carry position.
8

Leg carry.
9

Back carry, first step.

10

Back carry, final step.

11

12

13

14

Chapter 18
Bayonet Training

The bayonet symbolizes the will of the Marine to meet and destroy the enemy in hand-to-hand combat. This will is founded upon the Marine's confidence, courage, and determination, and is the result of vigorous training.

The bayonet is the weapon of silence and surprise. It is used at night during reconnaissance and infiltration missions, and whenever secrecy must be maintained. It is also used in close combat when the Marine and the enemy are too closely intermingled to permit the use of bullets or grenades. Then too, often a determined enemy cannot be dislodged by fire alone and must be driven from his position by hand-to-hand combat. This was often the situation with the fanatical Japanese soldiers defending the Pacific Islands that were invaded by the Marines in World War II.

The bayonet, or threat of the bayonet, can have a psychological effect on the enemy. This effect, combined with a mastery of the principles and movements of bayonet attack the Marine is taught in boot camp and beyond, all capped off with an aggressive spirit of attack, are the keys to success in combat with the bayonet.

We learned that, to begin with, there are three basic positions to take with the bayonet, described and illustrated below.

1. <u>The Guard Position</u>: To assume this position, face the enemy, place the left foot a short step forward and space the feet laterally, toes pointing toward the enemy. Bend the knees slightly and incline the body slightly forward as shown in the illustration below.

Guard.

This position allows the Marine to move swiftly in any direction to counter any movement by the enemy. At the same time, holding the rifle firmly with both hands, aggressively move it forward, pointing the bayonet at the enemy's throat. The rifle must be held firmly, but not rigidly, and without canting it to one side or the other. While balancing your weight on both legs and keeping your eyes on the enemy's bayonet and body, be ready for instant movement in any direction.

On the picture page at the end of the chapter picture 1 shows an instructor demonstrating the Guard position to recruits and pictures 2, 3, and 4 show my fellow recruits and myself assuming that position. In picture 4, the recruit to the far right is yours truly. Now don't you agree that if an enemy was confronted by such a lean, mean, fighting machine, he would drop his rifle and bayonet and run as fast as he could in the opposite direction?

On second thought, don't answer that question.

2. <u>The Short Guard Position</u>: To move from the Guard position to the Short Guard position, the Marine simply brings the rifle back so that the right hand is at the right hip as shown in the pictures 5 and 6. This is a handy rifle carrying position when moving through dense woods, ditches, and when around buildings, or when an enemy may suddenly be encountered at close quarters.

3. <u>High Port Position</u>: The High Port position is illustrated below.

High Port.

To assume the High Port position, carry the rifle diagonally across the body with the sling to the front and the left wrist level with, and in front of, the left shoulder. This too, along with the Guard position, enables the Marine to respond instantly to a sudden threat by the enemy.

<u>Basic Movements</u> with the bayonet: These are the basic tactics associated with hand-to-hand combat with the bayonet which we had to learn and become proficient in.

1. <u>The Whirl</u>: The Whirl is a rapid change of position to meet an attack coming from a different direction. From the position of Guard or Short Guard, bring the rifle to High Port and whirl to the left or right by pivoting on the ball of the leading foot; then resume the position of Guard to meet the new threat.

2. <u>The Long Thrust</u>: To perform the Long Thrust while in the Guard position:

a. Advance the rear foot and lunge forward, extending the whole body as shown in the two illustrations below.

Long Thrust (Positions at Beginning and End of Movement).

b. Grip the rifle firmly and guide it forcefully by the left hand in a straight line towards the enemy's throat or other open areas of his body. Incline the body well forward and extend the left arm to its full length to ensure the bayonet penetrates the target. Keep your eyes on the point of attack during the entire Long Thrust.

c. If the Long Thrust is evaded, follow up swiftly with another thrust or a butt stroke as defined below. Retraction recovery after the Long Thrust must be instantaneous, with no lingering in the extended position.

d. The force of the Long Thrust is determined by the arms, shoulders, back, legs and weight of the body. The distance from the enemy at which the Long Thrust is initiated depends on the reach and speed of advance of the attacker. It is vitally important for each Marine to know his reach and be able to judge his attack distance so that his thrust will have maximum effectiveness in penetrating the target. The maximum effective distance for each Marine is determined by trial and practice thrusting against the dummies as shown in picture 7.

3. <u>Withdrawal from the Long Thrust</u>: The following illustrations show Withdrawal from Long Thrust if the Long Thrust has been made with the right foot forward.

Withdrawal from Long Thrust.

    a. Move the left foot forward and jerk the rifle straight back along the line of penetration, moving the body to the rear by straightening out the forward leg. If necessary to maintain balance, shift the right foot to the rear.

    b. If the Long Thrust was made with the left foot leading, move the right foot forward and withdraw in the same manner as above. If the enemy is down, place one foot upon him and withdraw.

    c. In any event, withdraw instantly and be prepared to execute the Short Thrust or a Butt Stroke described in the following, or assume the position of Guard or Short Guard. Do not linger in the extended position.

    4. <u>Short Thrust and Withdrawal</u>: The Short Thrust is executed in the same manner as the Long Thrust except that the leading foot is advanced instead of the rear foot in lunging forward. The Short Thrust is necessary when an enemy is met suddenly at a distance too close for the Long Thrust. Withdrawal from the Short Thrust is the same as for the Long Thrust.

    5. <u>Parries</u>: The Parry is simply an offensive maneuver used to create an opening for a Short Thrust or Butt Stroke by forcing the enemy's bayonet out of the way. It consists of a forceful and swift forward and lateral movement of the attacker's bayonet as shown in the following illustration.

Parry Right.   Parry Left.

The lateral movement of the attacker's bayonet is limited to the extent necessary to move the enemy's blade clear of the attacker's body. There is a natural tendency to rotate the rifle while swiftly moving it in the lateral position. The attacker should avoid this since it will momentarily delay an immediate thrust after the parry.

a. The position of the enemy's weapon will determine the direction of the Parry, which obviously will be made in the direction that will immediately provide an opening for instant execution of a Short Thrust or Butt Stroke. If the opening allows for a Short Thrust, the Marine, at the instant his bayonet glances off the enemy's weapon, drives it into the enemy in the same continuous movement. Avoid the tendency to pull the bayonet back and then thrust it forward.

b. <u>Parry Right</u>: To Parry Right from the position of Guard, lunge forward as in a Long Thrust.

At the same time, thrust the rifle diagonally forward and to the right by straightening the left arm in the direction of the Parry, moving the butt of the rifle to the right and keeping the rifle parallel to the Guard position. Limit the diagonally forward movement only to the extent necessary to force the enemy's blade just clear of the Marine's body.

c. <u>Parry Left</u>: To Parry Left, the Marine lunges forward as in the Parry Right, thrusts his rifle forward and to the left so that the butt is approximately in front of his left groin, deflecting the opponent's bayonet clear of his body.

d. If the Parry Right or Parry Left does not bring the Marine's rifle on a line with the enemy's throat or body, or if he is too close to the enemy, he follows up with a butt stroke, which will hopefully momentarily disable the enemy, giving the Marine time to position himself for a long or a short thrust.

Pictures 8 and 9 show an instructor demonstrating parries and recruits practicing them.

6. <u>Vertical Butt Stroke</u>: To perform the Vertical Butt Stroke from the Guard position, as shown in the following illustration, step forward with the rear foot, while simultaneously driving the butt of the rifle forward and upward in a vertical arc to the groin, solar plexus, or chin of the enemy. Support the Vertical Butt Stroke with the force of the whole body.

Vertical Butt Stroke (Positions at Beginning and End of Movement).

    a. The Vertical Butt Stroke may also be initiated from a crouched position in order to hit low areas of the enemy's body while at the same time presenting him with a small difficult target.

    7. <u>Smash</u>: If the enemy moves backward, avoiding the Vertical Butt Stroke, the Marine steps forward quickly with the rear foot and drives the rifle butt at his head, extending the arms fully forward and advancing the rear foot as necessary to retain balance. The Smash movement is shown below.

Smash Following Vertical Butt Stroke.

    8. <u>Slash</u>: If the enemy again moves backward and the Smash movement fails to reach its target, the Marine continues to advance and Slash downward diagonally with the bayonet, aiming toward the juncture of the neck and shoulder. By aiming towards this point, the chances are that, if the Marine misses, the bayonet will strike the head, throat, or arms. The Slash movement is shown in the following illustration.

Slash Following Smash.

9. <u>Horizontal Butt Stroke</u>: With the Horizontal Butt Stroke, the plane of the rifle and bayonet is horizontal instead of vertical as in the Vertical Butt Stroke. The Horizontal Butt Stroke is shown below.

Horizontal Butt Stroke.

    a. To execute the Horizontal Butt Stroke from the Guard position, move in aggressively, advancing the rear foot and swinging the rifle butt diagonally upward through an arc to the enemy's head or body.

    b. If the Horizontal Butt Stroke misses, execute a Smash movement as previously described while keeping the butt of the rifle in the same horizontal position.

    c. If the Smash movement misses, continue to attack vigorously while executing a Slash movement as described previously. Picture 10 shows the recruit executing a Horizontal Butt Stroke.

    10. <u>Group Assault Tactics (Offensive)</u>: Group Assault Tactics are taught because when the Marine unit has a numerical advantage over the enemy unit, these tactics enable the Marines to

quickly gain an important advantage and rapidly decimate the enemy unit. For example, if two Marines confront one of the enemy and are able in a few seconds to put him out of action, they can quickly turn to another enemy. Such Group Assault Tactics executed in the initial critical seconds of meeting in hand-to-hand combat, may quickly reduce the enemy's initial strength by many men and have a devastating effect on the remainder of the enemy. On the other hand, Group Assault Tactics (Defensive) teach the Marine, when he is outnumbered, how best to repel the Group Assault Tactics employed by the enemy.

 a. <u>Offensive Two Against One</u>: As two Marine bayonet fighters approach a single enemy, they advance directly forward on a run, with neither one converging on the enemy. As they get within bayonet range, one of them directly confronts the enemy in a frontal attack. The other Marine quickly advances to the enemy's flank and then turns sharply to strike the enemy's exposed flank or rear.

 (1). If the enemy turns suddenly to fend off the flanking Marine's attack, he exposes himself to the Marine making the frontal attack, who then strikes instantly. This entire operation - approach, contact, and attack flows into one continuous assault and is completed in a few seconds.

 b. <u>Offensive Three Against Two</u>: Three Marines confront two of the enemy. They advance directly forward at a run. As the three Marines get within bayonet range, two of them engage the two enemy. The third Marine is then left momentarily free and proceeds to a point opposite the flank of the nearest enemy, veering suddenly towards that enemy and striking him in his exposed side, as in the two against one maneuver.

 (1). With one enemy disposed of, the remaining enemy is struck in the flank by either of the two Marines who can more quickly reach him.

 (2). If either enemy being attacked on his flank turns to defend himself, he leaves himself open to the Marine making the frontal assault.

 Offensive Group Assault Tactics, to be effective, must be simple and flexible, since it is impossible to predict what the exact scenario will be until the Marines are within close proximity to the enemy.

 11. <u>Group Assault Tactics (Defensive)</u>:

 a. <u>Defensive One Against Two</u>: When one Marine is confronted by two of the enemy, the Marine rushes forward keeping both enemies to one side of him, and under no circumstances allowing himself to be caught between them. Upon reaching the enemy, the Marine turns to the flank of the nearest enemy, keeping him between himself and the farther enemy. This enables the Marine to concentrate on disposing of one enemy at a time.

 b. <u>Defensive Two Against Three</u>: When two Marines are in contact with three of the enemy, they rush to the flanks of the two enemies on the sides, leaving the enemy in the center the last to be confronted. When one of the Marines has disposed of his opponent, he immediately attacks the remaining enemy.

 This concludes discussion on bayonet tactics. As I mentioned, we all thoroughly enjoyed bayonet training. I wonder if part of that enjoyment was if when we were butt stroking and shoving that bayonet into the dummy target we were imagining that the dummy target was the drill instructor. In summary, the bayonet is the ultimate form of combat in any assault. Success in combat with the bayonet depends on the mastery of the principles and movements just described, plus an aggressive spirit of attack on the part of the Marine and complete confidence in himself and his fellow Marines.

Finally, in combat it doesn't get any more personal than it does with the bayonet.

"The American Marines have pride and benefit from it. They are tough, cocky, sure of themselves and their buddies. They can fight and they know it."

General Mark Clark

5

6

7

8

9

10

Chapter 19
The Light at The End of The Tunnel

The light was finally bright at the end of that long twelve week tunnel of Marine Corps boot camp. We were a week from graduation and life became almost enjoyable again. Here again, the operative word is almost. There was no easing in the tough discipline or demand for perfection and instant obedience on the part of the Drill Instructors, nor a lessening of the harsh punishment when we failed to meet those demands. The change I'm speaking of was that the D.I.s became just a tad more personable in their treatment of us recruits. For example, they spoke to us more about what life in the Corps would be like after boot camp, the various specialties open to us, the opportunities for education and how to take advantage of those opportunities. They told us how to apply for training in any special branch we might be interested in such as maintenance, armor, aviation, reconnaissance, sniper, etc. To have a Drill Instructor speak to you as a fellow human being was truly a unique experience after eleven weeks of being spoken to as a maggot.

Then too, the D.I.s took us on a visit to the other side of the base, the side I mentioned in the beginning of the book, with the beautiful Spanish architecture, palm tree lined boulevards and manicured lawns, which was like a different planet compared to the recruit side of the base with its row upon row of quonset huts and drab scenery. The occasion for the visit was to get certain uniform items needed for graduation from the Base Exchange and to get our graduation pictures taken for the platoon yearbook. For the picture, each of us donned only the dress uniform white hat ("cover" in Marine lingo) and the dress uniform blue coat ("blouse" in Marine lingo) because the picture only covered us head to shoulders.

After eleven weeks of being surrounded only by recruits and Drill Instructors, the reader can imagine how enjoyable it was for us recruits to be shopping in that base exchange filled with regular people and a vast array of assorted merchandise. Also, in front of the base exchange, was a large patio type area with benches as shown as picture 1 on the picture page.

SDI Beeson had lit the smoking lamp. Let me tell you that sitting outside on a bench in that patio area, enjoying a leisurely smoke in the warm sun, gorgeous scenery, and watching a crowd of people other than recruits of various races, ethnicities, colors, and shapes -especially the ladies - passing by, was just a little bit of paradise. But of course, it all had to end too soon. After everyone had made their purchases and had their picture taken, the Drill Instructors called us into formation and marched us back across the parade field to the recruit area of the base.

Nevertheless, that time at the Base Exchange when we shed the maggot status and rejoined the human race even for a brief time, whet our appetite for graduation when we would shed the maggot status and rejoin the human race for good.

The last week of boot camp was almost entirely filled with practicing formation drill and performing the manual of arms while marching. It was tradition that, during the graduation ceremony, the Drill Instructors of each graduating platoon would have a set time to lead their platoon through a routine of manual of arms formation drill. It was an opportunity for the D.I.s to show the commanding officers of the base and the families of the recruits and other attending dignitaries their expertise in turning a bunch of raw recruits who didn't know their left foot from their right into a disciplined military unit of precision, unity and excellence. And naturally, each set of D.I.s wanted their platoon to outperform the others. Given this, that week of manual of arms formation drill prior to graduation was intense to put it mildly. SDI Beeson and JDI Chapman viewed it as competition drill - competition with those other D.I.s and their platoons.

Even minor mistakes were considered as major by our D.I.s, and strongly criticized with the reminder that, with all the drill formation we had practiced during the previous eleven weeks, even so-called minor mistakes were inexcusable at this point. And we needed to be reminded that, in the Marines, there is no such thing as a minor mistake. I'm sure that some of those mistakes didn't even happen but were products of the D.I.'s imagination so they could reapply the standard demand for perfection. Why? Because I'm sure they sensed in us a tendency to ease up on the pressure of always striving for that perfection since we were so close to graduation, and they were determined to rid us of that tendency before it could take hold. At any rate, when that week of drill practice was completed, we were thoroughly confident that we would excel in performing that graduation drill routine. And we did!

It was at this time that I was informed by SDI Beeson that I and one other recruit out of our platoon would be promoted to Private First Class on graduation day. My performance as Right Guide of the platoon for nearly the whole time of boot camp was the basis for my promotion. The other recruit who was promoted with me was exceptionally sharp with outstanding grades and performance in all the training classes and exercises. SDI Beeson informed us that our promotions out of boot camp qualified us to attend Sea School, an assignment highly desired and open to only a few of the sharpest recruit graduates. Sea School entailed two to three weeks of training, after which we as PFCs could expect sea duty as an Admiral's or ship Captain's Marine orderly, messenger, and aide. Picture 2 shows a Marine PFC orderly delivering a message to a ship's Captain.

Training consisted of military and naval etiquette, the duties of orderlies and messengers aboard ship, duties during emergency drills at sea and, of course, actual emergencies, and learning a multitude of new terms, such as ships have decks rather than floors, overheads instead of ceilings, bulkheads instead of walls, galleys instead of kitchens, and scuttlebutts instead of fountains. Additionally, the direction right is starboard, and the direction left is port. Permission to smoke aboard ship was announced with the words, "The smoking lamp is lit," a phrase we were familiar with since it was used by the D.I.s in boot camp.

A sharp appearance, fitness, and a generally tough demeanor were the desired traits exhibited when one represented the Marine Corps. Navy ships made port calls around the world, and you could be the first and only Marine the locals would ever see, not counting John Wayne in the movies. So, spit-shined, polished, and squared away were the inflexible standards associated with Sea School and subsequent sea duty as shown in the following illustration.

    The custom of Marines as orderlies for flag officers and ship's Captains of the Navy goes back to the formation of the Continental Marines in 1775. Over the years, the Marine orderly aboard Navy ships became almost a part of Naval tradition.

    My friend and I were initially enthused over the opportunity. After all, what was there not to like about a cushy job as an Admiral's or Captain's orderly and a chance to see the world. But then we were informed that the two to three weeks of Sea School were essentially an additional two to three weeks of boot camp, and in some respects even tougher, because of the standards. Well, that put a complete damper on our enthusiasm. We both agreed that there was no way on God's green earth that we were going to experience a day more of boot camp life than absolutely necessary. Then too, for me, there was my overriding desire to be a fighter pilot and a couple years of sea duty would put that desire on hold. And so, we both turned down the opportunity to attend Sea School.

    The remaining days to graduation passed slowly and were finally behind us, and as I said, when that last day of formation drill was finished, we were absolutely convinced that we had reached the standard of perfection set by the Drill Instructors, and we had nothing more to learn about formation drill and the Manuel of Arms. It was a bit intimidating to realize that we soon would be exiting the gate of the Marine Corps Recruit Depot and reentering the wide, wide world. We would be free of the absolute, total control of every aspect of our lives by the Drill Instructors over the past twelve weeks, and now free to make our own decisions. I think our feeling was somewhat akin to that of a prisoner who had served his sentence and was now a free man. We were looking forward to a ten day leave granted to boot camp graduates, going home to family and friends and basking in their admiration and respect, and for some, even envy of our elevated status as a United States Marine. As for me, I was looking forward to seeing those who had said that I was too small and spindly to be a Marine and showing them that I not only had what it took, but I had excelled by being promoted out of boot camp.

    The day before graduation was spent getting our uniforms, shoes, and rifles ready for inspection. Our uniforms were ironed to perfection with the three creases on the back of the shirt sharp and located precisely. The globe and anchor emblems on the collars were also precisely located, as well as the rifle qualification badge and the pistol qualification badge just above the left breast pocket. The belt buckle was polished to a brilliant shine. And the shoes were polished, and spit shined. And by the way, that term "spit-shined" was literal in its meaning. After getting the best shine possible with the polish, you would spit on the front of the shoes or boots and use the brush and rag to buff them to an even greater shine. Picture 3 shows a recruit doing this.

    As I got into bed that night before graduation, I realized that it was the last time I would be sleeping in a bunk bed in a concrete World War II quonset hut. With a ten day leave coming up,

I would soon be sleeping again in my comfortable bed at home in Nebraska -that is, if my parents hadn't sold my bed after I left for boot camp. With that thought, along with the familiar sound of jets taking off from nearby Lindberg Airport, I fell asleep.

"Courage is endurance for one moment more."

Unknown Marine 2nd Lieutenant in Vietnam

1

2

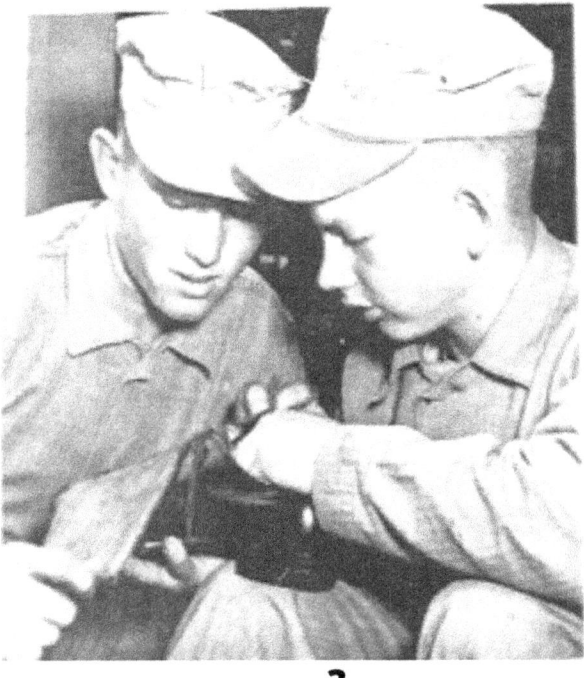

3

Chapter 20
Graduation

It was a day of pomp and ceremony which no one does better than the United States Marine Corps. It was also a day filled with a sense of pride, fulfillment, and enormous satisfaction at having completed that twelve weeks of insult, challenge, physical and mental suffering involved in the transformation from civilian to maggot to Marine. The thrill of the pomp and ceremony of graduation and the realization that boot camp was over and our time as maggots was coming to an end forced all memories of the toughness and harshness of boot camp to fade into the background.

The Marine Recruit Depot band marched on to the parade field looking splendid in their dress blues, shown in picture 1 on the picture page. In addition to the National Anthem and the Marine Corps Hymn, the band would play historical marching music for the graduating platoons to show their stuff before the reviewing officials and the attending audience. Let me digress for a moment to insert an interesting historical note.

Among those famous marching compositions, the Recruit Depot band played that day was *The Stars and Stripes Forever*, composed by John Philip Sousa, one of the most famous directors of the official United States Marine Corps Band from 1880 to 1892. The Marine Corps Band, stationed in Washington D.C. and commonly known as "The President's Own," was established by an act of Congress in 1798, and remains today as one of the most elite musical groups in the country. And John Philip Sousa's *The Stars and Stripes Forever* was named the "Official March of the United States" in 1987 and is the best known and beloved march music in American history.

Following the Recruit Depot Band on to the parade field were the graduating recruit platoons, one shown in picture 2 with rifles at right shoulder arms, each column file aligned perfectly and everyone in step with the Drill Instructor's cadence. The graduating platoons would form up in front of the reviewing stand and reviewing officials as shown in picture 3 with the audience bleachers behind the reviewing stand.

Picture 4 shows SDI Beeson marching our platoon towards our position in front of the reviewing stand. As a contrast, the bottom two pictures 5 and 6 shows SDI Beeson marching us from the receiving barracks to the recruit area of the base 12 weeks earlier, showing the dramatic transformation from maggot to Marine.

The following pictures are of our platoon taking its turn marching in the competition drill with the other graduating platoons. The two pictures 7 and 8 show us establishing proper spacing between individuals in each column. Upon the command to take spacing, each individual except the one at the end places their left hand on their left hip which extends their elbow. They then move towards the individual on their left until their elbow is touching them. While doing this, they keep their head turned toward that individual. This is the proper spacing. Upon the command, "Ready, Front!" they smartly move their arm down and their head facing forward. Proper spacing is established. As indicated by the word "smartly," all movements are done swiftly and precisely.

The rifle is held at the right side with the butt on the ground while doing this. This position is called "Order Arms."

We were required to perform the manual of arms while marching in front of the reviewing officials. This gave them a chance to evaluate our expertise as graduates as well as the Drill Instructors' talents in training us. The manual of arms requires moving the rifle smartly and precisely from right shoulder arms to left shoulder arms, from left shoulder arms to right shoulder arms, to in-trail arms, to port arms, to salute arms, and all this while maintaining the proper spacing and keeping in perfect step with the Drill Instructor's cadence. The following pictures show us at the various stages mentioned.

The sequence in pictures 9 and 10 show us going from a position of order arms where the rifle is at the Marine's right side with the butt on the ground, as shown in the previous picture 8, to a position of right shoulder arms. The Marine smartly raises the rifle with the right hand to a position diagonally across the front of his body, while at the same time grabbing the rifle with his left hand as shown in picture 9. With his right hand on the butt of the rifle, he then moves the rifle to his right shoulder while rotating it to place it there, as shown in picture 10. The completed maneuver is shown in picture 11, with yours truly at the head of the formation as right guide.

If a hand salute is required while in this position, it is given as shown in picture 12 with the left arm snapped crosswise to the body and the palm of the left hand touching the top of the rifle in the bolt area.

Pictures 13 and 14 show us going from right shoulder arms to left shoulder arms. The Marine lifts the rifle off his right shoulder, rotates it, grabs the front hand guard with his left hand, and the small of the stock with his right hand. He smartly moves the rifle to his left shoulder as shown. He then grabs the butt of the rifle with his left hand and moves his right arm back to his right side. Pictures 15 and 16 show us marching at left shoulder arms.

Picture 17 shows us marching with our rifles in the "in-trail position." Picture 18 shows us with our rifles at the "present arms" position, which is how you salute a person when you are standing still at attention with your rifle at your side at "order arms" and then given the order "Present Arms." You lift the rifle, holding it directly in front of you while at attention.

We did our manual of arms drill march routine in front of the reviewing officials without making any mistakes, at least not any that were noticeable. In fact, SDI Beeson and JDI Chapman seemed quite pleased with our performance. And with that, graduation ended, and I'll close this account with two pictures - picture 19 of a warrior for whom I have deep respect - Senior Drill Instructor Beeson, and picture 20 of the recruit from the Midwest who his relatives and others thought was too small and skinny to be a Marine marching at the head of the platoon as its Right Guide and one of two distinguished graduates of that platoon - PFC Darrell Ahrens.

We marched back to the barracks, cleaned out our wall lockers and foot lockers, finished packing our duffel bags, and stripped the bunks of bedding and folded sheets and blanket nicely and left them on top of the bunks to be picked up later. We said farewell to the Drill Instructors and proceeded to the transportation office on the other side of the parade field to catch a bus that would take us to our point of departure - whether the bus station, train station, or airport. In my case, it was the train station, from which I would enjoy a two-day train ride to Columbus, Nebraska from where I had departed 12 weeks prior.

Remember my comment about the attractive lady on the train who said I was the sharpest looking military man in my uniform among all the others on the train. Picture 21 is of me in the tan uniform I was wearing when she made her comment. Picture 22 is of me in the dress blue uniform, also while on leave. The handsome young man with me in both pictures is my little brother Galen.

It was with a mixture of relief, pride, and joy that we exited the gates of Marine Corps Recruit Depot which we had entered 12 weeks before with mixed feelings of anxiety, fear, and trepidation. We had entered those gates as civilians, were tagged as maggots while we were there, and now exited those gates as members of that long line of the few, the proud, the Marines. The following picture is our graduation photo. I am in the first row, third from the left.

> *Here's to the Marine who guards our nation's shores;*
> *Here's to the Marine who guards heaven's doors.*
> *Here's to the Marine whose devotion measured full;*
> *Here's to the Marine whose devotion fills that measure still.*
> *So, my fellow Marines, let us lift our glasses high,*
> *In a solemn toast to the next Marine to die.*
>
> **SEMPER FI**

1

2

3

4

5

6

— LEATHERNECK —

7

8

9

10

11

12

13

14

15

16

17

18

"Mess with one Marine and you will mess with them all."

The Marine Brotherhood

Postscript

I would like to mention two of the many memorable events that occurred during my tour of active duty in the Marines after boot camp. I managed to serve my tour without getting into serious trouble, except for these two occasions which had the potential for trouble of the worst kind. The reader will recall that I mentioned in the narrative that being sent to the Brig was a major fear of every Marine. The Brig was the term for the Marine prison for serious offenses. Treatment of prisoners was rumored to be severe, very severe. My two events were serious violations of the Uniform Code of Military Justice, one my being Absent Without Official Leave (AWOL), and the other sleeping on guard duty. Each of the two offenses could be punished by court-martial and three to six months in the Brig. Only the kindness and understanding of the circumstances of each event by a couple of Gunnery Sergeants resulted in my avoiding a court-martial and time in the Brig.

Both events occurred while I was stationed at Marine Corps Base, 29 Palms, California. The AWOL event occurred during a weekend liberty In Los Angeles. Nick, a fellow Marine in the unit, owned a car and would go to Los Angeles during weekend liberty to visit his girlfriend. He offered rides to any of his buddies who wanted to go to L.A. for their weekend liberty. He would drop his buddies off at the L.A. bus depot on Friday afternoon and pick them up there on Sunday afternoon for the ride back to 29 Palms. I took advantage of this on a few occasions.

On one of those weekends, I decided on Saturday afternoon to hitchhike to Long Beach, a fairly short distance, and visit the amusement park located near the beach. While In Long Beach, I called Nick's girlfriend's house to inform Nick that on Sunday afternoon he should pick me up at the Long Beach bus depot instead of in L.A. Nick wasn't there, but his girlfriend's mother assured me that she would give Nick the message. Well, she forgot to do so.

I went to the Long Beach bus depot Sunday afternoon to await Nick's arrival. I stretched out on one of the depot's benches near the front entrance to the depot, knowing that if Nick or one of his passengers came inside to get me, they couldn't help but see me. And you guessed it - I fell asleep. As I slept soundly in the Long Beach bus depot, Nick and the others were thoroughly searching the Los Angeles bus depot for me. I was told later that, after a long fruitless search, they eventually had to get on the road if they were going to get back to the base at a reasonable hour.

I awoke around 6:30 a.m. Monday morning, and it was panic time. Morning formation and roll call at the base was held at 08:00 hours as I recall, and if I wasn't there, I would officially be classified as AWOL. There was a bus leaving for 29 Palms shortly and I desperately wanted to get on it. The bus ride from Long Beach to 29 Palms, as I recall, was 1hr.30min. I would still be late for roll call, but that was far less serious than being AWOL. But there was another problem. I was 15 cents short of the price of the bus ticket. I tried to negotiate with the ticket seller to no avail. I approached passengers in the bus depot asking them for 15 cents, even offering to repay them through the mail to no avail. I then went out to the sidewalk in front of the bus depot, stopped pedestrians, explained my dilemma, and asked if they could give a Marine 15 cents. Well, no one wanted to give me the time of the day, much less 15 cents.

I finally realized that trying to get back to 29 Palms on my own was a futile endeavor, and the best thing I could do was turn myself in to the local Navy/Marine military police, the Shore Patrol. I got the number of the local Shore Patrol office, called them, informed them of who I was and my situation, and was told to stay where I was, and someone would pick me up shortly. It wasn't long before a military police vehicle showed up with two shore patrol officers, one who asked me if I was the Marine who made the call, and when I confirmed it, he informed me that I was under arrest. The other was there to guard me in case I changed my mind and tried to escape.

We proceeded to the Navy Shore Patrol office and a clerk began filling out the paperwork charging me with being AWOL, informing 29 Palms of my location, and arranging for my return. A Navy Petty Officer, bless him, told that clerk, to be sure to include the fact that I had turned myself in to the Shore Patrol. With that, the Navy Shore Patrol informed the Marine detachment in Long Beach of my status and requested they send a guard to come and take me to the Marine Barracks. Two big, mean-looking Marines showed up, one carrying a loaded M-1 rifle. His duty was to stay close to me with that rifle ready for instant use. There was no doubt in my mind what the outcome would be if I tried to escape.

Upon arrival at the Marine barracks, I assumed I could get some sleep while arrangements were being made to get me back to 29 Palms. How naive of me! I and some other prisoners who were there were given work dungarees to change into and an entrenching tool to dig with, taken to an area of the Marine compound overgrown with thick weeds and scrub-brushes, and told to start pulling and digging to clear the area. It was hard work and after two hours or so, another prisoner and I were called out, taken back to the barracks, given back our civilian clothes and told to change and get ready to be taken to the bus depot. Upon arrival, my fellow prisoner and I were escorted on to the bus by our armed guard who then exited the bus and we departed for 29 Palms.

Although my fellow prisoner was based at 29 Palms, he was in a different unit, and we had never met. He wasn't open to conversation, and neither was I, although I was curious as to the seriousness of his offense. I was soon to be informed of it. The bus stopped in San Bernardino for a rest stop and bathroom break. Both of us exited the bus and headed for the men's room. On the way back to the bus, he stopped, told me that he would not be getting back on the bus, and wished me good luck. When I asked him why he was not going to return to base, he explained that this AWOL was only one of a number of offenses he would be charged with, that he would certainly face court-martial, and at least six months and probably more in the Brig. And that he was determined to avoid, even if it meant being on the run and eventually leaving the country.

I tried to talk him out of it, told him that even if he left the country, as a deserter he would be subject to arrest if he ever returned to the States since there is no Statute of Limitations on desertion, and the punishment for that would be far worse than what he now faced. All to no avail. He told me to tell base authorities at 29 Palms that we got separated in the depot, that I returned to the bus, but he never showed up, and the bus driver said he could not wait while I conducted a search for him, and he would leave me there if I exited the bus. I often wondered what happened to him.

When I returned, I was ordered to report to the Battalion Gunnery Sergeant. I was really scared as I headed to the Gunny's office since, as I mentioned, being AWOL, according to the

Uniform Code of Military Justice, carried a potential punishment of court-martial and time in the Brig. In fact, we had had a Marine in our unit who applied for emergency leave to attend his grandfather's funeral. Apparently, he and his grandfather had a very close relationship, and he desperately wanted to be there for his funeral. I forget the reason, but his request for emergency leave was turned down. He went AWOL to attend the funeral, and then returned to base. He was sentenced to court-martial and time in the Brig. In fact, I was assigned prisoner guard duty at his court-martial, and really felt sorry for him. Remembering that increased my fears over what was in store for me.

I reported to the Gunnery Sergeant, stood at attention, and sweat bullets while awaiting his judgment. He was from Arkansas and had a reputation for being tough but fair. After a long pause, he gave me "at ease." He then informed me that my good record as a Marine, the fact that I had never violated the Corps' rules and regulations before, and that I demonstrated good sense and judgment by reporting myself AWOL to the Shore Patrol, all weighed heavily in my favor. Therefore, there would be no disciplinary action taken against me. But he followed that up with a warning that if I ever committed a similar offense in the future and appeared before him, he would throw the book at me. And with that, he dismissed me. And I, snapping to attention with a hearty "Yes Sir," did an about face and exited his office with a gigantic sense of relief.

The second event, which in the Marine Code of Conduct was an even more serious offense than my being AWOL, occurred while on board a naval vessel during an amphibious landing exercise. The reader will recall that I referred to this exercise previously in the chapter on Physical Training and discussion of the rope ladder. Picture 1 shows me on deck of the vessel off the coast of California taking in the sea breeze and trying to fight off seasickness.

My offense occurred while taking my turn on guard duty in the hold of the ship which contained the equipment and vehicles that would be going ashore with us. The ship was a flat bottom vessel with the area containing the cargo I was guarding located at the waterline. Picture 2 shows the type of ship referred to.

While I was on guard duty, we were experiencing a period of exceptionally rough seas. Being at the waterline, every time a large wave would slam the bow of that ship, it would send a strong compression shock throughout the cargo hold. The equipment and vehicles were chained down and couldn't move. But I wasn't, and more than a few times, I was knocked off my feet. I thought to myself, "Why am I walking around this compartment and getting knocked on my rear?" With the entire compartment enclosed, all I had to do was find a spot where I had clear view of the entire area I was guarding and everything in it and stay there. I could have control over the entire area while avoiding walking around and being knocked down. I found that sweet spot in the front seat of one of the jeeps.

Well, you can guess what happened! Apparently, I didn't realize how exhausted I was, because when I relaxed in that seat, it wasn't long before I was fast asleep. The next thing I felt was a strong hand on my shoulder, shaking me, and a rough voice ordering me to wake up. That hand and voice belonged to the Marine Sergeant of the Guard. I sat up, responded "Yes Sir!" scrambled out of that jeep and snapped to attention. He asked me if I could stay awake for the remainder of my tour of guard duty. When I replied, "Yes Sir!" he ordered me to stay on my feet and report to him when I finished my tour of guard duty.

The reader will recall, in the chapter entitled "The Marine Guard," my comments regarding the dire consequences for a Marine on guard duty who violated any one of the eleven general orders of guard duty we had to memorize. Well, by falling asleep in the seat of that jeep, I could immediately recall at least three of those general orders I not only had totally violated, but decimated. Those were:

1. To walk my post in a military manner, with the discipline, attention to detail, and readiness to respond to any danger required of a Marine guard.

2. To stay alert and be aware of all that is occurring in my area of responsibility.

3. To properly challenge and identify all who enter my area of responsibility and respond as appropriate.

To say I was scared would be an understatement. My heart sank as I considered the possible consequences of my offense - a Summary Court Martial, reduction in rank to Private, and up to six months in the Brig. Also, with that Court Martial, a General, or even Dishonorable Discharge was in the realm of possibility. I had the remainder of my tour of guard duty in the hold of that ship to mull over those disastrous possibilities. And thinking back on it, I'm sure that is precisely what that Sergeant of the Guard had in mind when he allowed me to finish my tour of guard duty. He wanted me to experience the fear and panic that went with considering the consequences of my action.

Well, I reported to the Sergeant of the Guard after I was relieved from guard duty. I don't remember all he said, but he reminded me in strong terms of the seriousness of my offense. He emphasized that the reason the Corps took such an offense so seriously was that, in a combat situation, such a failure could result not only in the death of the offender, but in that of his fellow Marines. Therefore, in keeping with the Marine philosophy of "no excuse" for any failure, he reminded me that, even if I were being knocked on my ass with every wave that hit that ship, with the possibility of physical injury, it did not excuse me from violating general orders by taking a seat in that jeep. He asked if I understood that, and what punishment I could be subject to. I acknowledged my guilt and said I understood both the seriousness and the possible consequences.

After a pause, a long pause, he said that he was satisfied that I understood both the seriousness of my offense and the potential punishment. He also said that he didn't want to ruin the clean record of a good Marine by reporting my offense to higher authorities. However, the fact remained that I had violated a cardinal rule and regulation associated with guard duty. Therefore, there must be punishment for my offense. After some thought, he informed me that I would be assigned to mess duty for the next day from early morning to evening.

The reader will recall my comment of how we recruits hated that week of mess duty while at Camp Matthews. Well, mess duty aboard ship was even harder work and more messy (pardon the pun) than on land. But considering the alternative of what the Uniform Code of Military Justice recommended as punishment for sleeping on guard duty, I considered a day of shipboard mess duty a sign from heaven. I silently called down a blessing on that Marine Sergeant of the Guard.

"It was the Marines who taught me how to act.

After that, pretending to be tough wasn't so hard."

Lee Marvin

1

2

Addendum

My hopes to attend pilot training in the Marine Corps did not come about. Following boot camp and after combat training at Camp Pendleton, California I was assigned to Marine Corps Base Twenty Nine Palms as a radio operator in a 155 mm. Howitzer artillery battalion as part of the combat ready Fleet Marine Force. When my enlistment term was about to end, the Gunnery Sergeant called me in and said, "Ahrens, you've been a good Marine, and the battalion commander is pleased with your performance as his radio operator. We would like you to re-enlist." The Gunnery Sergeant also mentioned that he knew from my records that I had applied for pilot training and that I had passed the requirements for entrance into that program. He said, "Re-enlist and we'll see what we can do to send you to Pensacola Florida for flight training." I replied, "Give me orders to pilot training and then I'll re-enlist," whereupon Gunny replied, "No! You have to re-enlist first." And with that, I accepted my honorable discharge, and my active duty tour in the Marines ended.

I returned home, worked a number of jobs, re-entered college, and eventually received an officer's commission and appointment to pilot training in the Air Force. My enlisted time in the Marines put me a few years behind my fellow officers in the Air Force, so the question arises, "Did I regret those years in the Marines?" And the answer is, "No! Absolutely not!" That saying, "Once a Marine, always a Marine" is true. Also, there seems to be a little bit of extra respect given those in the Corps. I noticed this from my fellow officers and pilots when they found out that I was a former enlisted Marine. Then too, as I mentioned before, as Right Guide of our Recruit Platoon, I learned some important lessons of leadership, the hard way. And being an officer with prior enlisted experience proved to be an advantage when dealing with subordinates. So, the bottom line is that I am very grateful for my experience being one of the few, the proud, a Marine.

An example of that extra bit of respect given a Marine which I mentioned above occurred when I came before a review board led by a high-ranking Air Force officer who were deciding whether or not I would be accepted for commissioning as an officer in the Air Force and selection for pilot training. After being notified of my acceptance and selection, I asked the review board president if I would have to go through basic training in the Air Force. He laughed and replied, "Ahrens, anyone who has gone through Marine Corps boot camp has nothing to learn from any other service's basic training."

The expression "Once a Marine, always a Marine" is reflected in the statement of Lee Marvin who I quoted, who said that because of his time in the Marines, he had no problem acting tough in the movies. It came natural to him. Many recognize Lee Marvin as a famous movie actor who won numerous awards, including the Academy Award for his roles mostly as a tough guy in some 48 movies, but few probably know that, as a Marine decorated for valor in World War II, he participated in many of the invasions of Japanese held islands in the Pacific, including Saipan where he was seriously wounded, requiring hospitalization back in the States for nearly a year.

After the war, release from the Marines, and recovery from his wounds, he took up his acting career.

Lee Marvin made it clear that he was prouder of the fact that he was a U.S. Marine than of the fame and wealth he gained as an actor. The headstone of his grave at Arlington National Cemetery reads simply, "Lee Marvin, PFC, U.S. Marine Corps, World War II."

In my reminiscences of my boot camp experiences over sixty years ago, I couldn't help but consider the state of our military today. Back then we had the draft. Today we have the All-Volunteer Military. I ask the reader's indulgence while I use this addendum to share my insight and opinions on the effects this change from a conscription type military to an all-volunteer military has had on the military, the nation, its people, our society and culture, and its international perception. I feel I have a right to state my opinions given 26 1/2 years of service as an enlisted Marine, Air Force officer, and fighter pilot. This addendum can therefore be considered as my treatise on the All-Volunteer Military Force.

The year 2023 marked the 50th anniversary of the All-Volunteer Military Force, which came about primarily as a result of the Vietnam War. The extensive civil protests against the Vietnam War, with its increasing casualties and expenditure of resources, reached their climax in the violence accompanying the Democratic National Convention of 1968, which gave impetus to an already existing political effort to end selective service and the draft. The Gates Commission was established to conduct a study and develop options for doing this. As it turned out, the Gates Commission strongly recommended that the draft be discontinued and the nation move on to an All-Volunteer Military Force, which was supported by President Nixon, the majority of Congress and the military, as well as a majority of the American people.

Over the years, the All-Volunteer Military has been highly praised for its high degree of professionalism, combat effectiveness, and public support. Nevertheless, almost since its inception, it has had its major critics who have identified serious disadvantages associated with an All-Volunteer Military, disadvantages which have grown more serious over the years, and which today are approaching critical mass. Let us review some of these disadvantages.

One major disadvantage of the All-Volunteer Military is the effect that cultural changes have had on its readiness, and particularly as those cultural changes have affected the population of young adults, which in turn affect the enlistment rates crucial to the sustainability of the All-Volunteer Military.

In a document written in 2006, Bernard Rostker, senior Rand Corporation fellow, stated the following: "In 1969, four years before the United States eliminated the draft and moved to an All-Volunteer Military, a member of the President's Commission on an All-Volunteer Force wrote the chairman that 'While there is a reasonable possibility that a peacetime armed force could be entirely voluntary, I am certain that an armed force involved in a major conflict could not be voluntary.'"

Mr. Rostker went on to say that rising casualties from the Global War on Terror, multiple long overseas combat deployments, dropping enlistments, the deteriorating situation in Iraq, and a majority of the American public no longer believing that the war is worth fighting, make the issue of recruiting enough volunteers to maintain the U.S. military force at required levels extremely critical. Keep in mind that this document was distributed in 2006, showing that even back then, there were serious doubts concerning the sustainability of the All-Volunteer Military.

In his blog article dated July 18, 2023, Erin M. Staine-Pyne states that the year 2023 marked two events - the 50th anniversary of the United States All-Volunteer Military, and at the same time, one of the worst recruiting years for the U.S. military since 1973. He also claims that one of the primary causes for this is that the country today has a population of young adults who are less informed, less interested, and less qualified for military service. But an even greater concern than this is the fact that a majority of our young population does not see the value of military service or feel any obligation to serve in the defense of their country.

Various military and civilian organizational statistics bear this out. The population of potential recruits continues to decline because of criminal records, drug use, obesity, and the inability to qualify intellectually - that is, pass the service entrance exam. Recent testimony given before Congress revealed that only 23 percent of American youth ages 17 to 24 are qualified to serve in the military without a waiver. To make the crisis even worse is the fact that, according to an internal Defense Department survey, only 9 percent of those 23 percent eligible to serve in the military have any inclination to do so.

Every year the Pentagon must recruit approximately 150,000 service members to keep the All-Volunteer Military Force viable. The most productive age group for the recruiters to recruit from is the group of 18 year old high school graduates. Every year, approximately 4 million American youth turn 18, and applying the 23 percent statistic concerning those who are able to meet the minimum enlistment standards, that leaves 920,000 able to serve. However, applying the 9 percent of those willing to serve, leaves approximately 83,000 who are both able and willing to serve.

Since the yearly requirement for recruits is 150,000, but the availability of recruits from the most likely pool of candidates who are both able and willing to serve is 83,000, there is a possible shortfall of 67,000 enlistments needed to maintain the All-Volunteer Military at required levels. The possibility of making up this shortfall through enlistments of other age groups is extremely remote, if not impossible altogether. This clearly poses a risk to national security; yet there are many who still deny there is a serious problem with the All-Volunteer Military, including those in the White House, the Congress, the military, and the general public. And keep in mind the fact that the requirement for 67,000 additional enlistments is for keeping a peacetime All-Volunteer Force up to strength, not a wartime All-Volunteer Force.

Maj. Gen. (Ret) Dennis Laich and Col. (Ret) Lawrence Wilkerson, in their column entitled *America's All-Volunteer Force is in Crisis - and Denial*, dated August 10, 2022, make the point that these shortfalls in enlistments exist in spite of extraordinary measures established over the past decade to attract recruits. The Army and Air Force offered unprecedented enlistment bonuses of up to $50,000 and the Navy up to $25,000. The Army, for the first time, offered recruits their first duty station of choice. Also, the longstanding recruit qualifications were reviewed by the Army with an eye toward lowering them. This included considering a temporary suspension of the requirement for a high school diploma or GED, but under severe protests, this was rejected.

The Global War on Terror, with its longstanding commitments in Afghanistan and Iraq, accentuated the shortfalls of the All-Volunteer Military. By 2010, more than two million service members had been deployed, with 43 percent serving multiple deployments. It wasn't long before the negative impact of repeated deployments on the physical, mental, and emotional health of service members and their families became apparent.

The Army, in its attempt to make up for its manpower shortages, implemented a stop-loss policy which allowed the selective prevention of troops from leaving the service, despite their having completed their voluntary commitment and after having completed at least one combat tour. This basically amounted to involuntary servitude. The Army also recalled numerous separated soldiers back to active duty.

Not long ago, the Pentagon acknowledged that recruiting shortfalls for 2022 were alarming, and that impending shortfalls for future years appear to be just as alarming, if not more so. Lt. Gen. (Ret) Thomas Spoehr of the Heritage Foundation has said that "this is the start of a long drought for military recruiting." He went on to emphasize that, in large numbers, young people are simply not inclined to join the military. All the services are struggling to attract new recruits, despite the offers of generous signing bonuses and, in the case of the Army, relaxed entrance requirements.

As mentioned before, long before the Global War on Terror began on September 11, 2001, voices were warning of major problems with the All-Volunteer Military. In the September 1997 issue of the geopolitical / military publication *Proceedings*, Maj. Gen. (Ret) J.D. Lynch, USMC, stated that the All-Volunteer Force had reached critical mass, and it was time to sound reveille. The General said that the social fabric of the U.S. Military was showing signs of wear, and that this should not come as any real surprise since the society from which it springs is also showing signs of serious decay, and that a chat with high-school teachers and police officers serving in any medium - sized or larger city should give strong indication of the depth of the decay.

Keep in mind that General Lynch made his comments in 1997, 26 years ago, and since then conditions have only gotten worse. The General said that any thinking person need not wonder why society is decaying and a high percentage of modern youth lack core values that were prevalent in youth as recently as in the 1950s. And the sad truth is that the lack of these core values extends far beyond youth into the population as a whole. Furthermore, this decline in the core values of Judeo - Christianity upon which our Founding Fathers built this nation has had a disastrous effect on virtually every aspect of our culture and society, just as our Founding Fathers predicted it would, if we became so foolish as to set aside these core values. Let's consider the General's comments in light of today's realities.

In the 1950s, the average share of the population that attended church on a regular basis was in the 70 percent range. Today, that figure is in the 30 percent range. In the 1950s, the public education system of the U.S. was the envy of the world. However, since the 1960s when prayer, references to the Bible, and the teaching of core values in the classroom was prohibited for fear of offending some segment of society, the public education system, to a large extent, has become a scandal and embarrassment, with America's students proficiency in math, science, and the liberal arts, far, far, below that of many nations, in some cases ranking as far down as number 28 compared to other nations.

In the 1950s, our universities and colleges were bastions of learning, free speech and dialogue, and scholarship. Today, with a minority of exceptions, the majority, including especially the so-called ivy league institutions, are bastions of radical leftist liberalism, socialism, and anti-Americanism. In the 1950s, America was a law-abiding nation, with police given high respect and support. Today, America is suffering a nation-wide crime wave and police, especially in our major cities, are insulted, attacked, and unsupported.

In the 1950s, a military service obligation to the country was just assumed by a majority of the youthful population. I can attest to this since I enlisted in the Marines in 1956. Today, as stated, only 9 percent of young adults feel any such obligation. The emphasis of too many today is on what benefits they can get from their country, rather than on what service they can give to their country in gratitude for the vast freedoms and opportunities the country gives them. The call of President John F. Kennedy in the early 60s to "Ask not what your country can do for you; ask what you can do for your country," has been flipped to read: "Ask not what you can do for your country; ask what your country can do for you."

Jason Dempsey and Gil Barndollar in their blog entitled, *The All-Volunteer Force is in Crisis*, claim that the All-Volunteer Military gives most Americans the freedom to be indifferent to their military obligation, shifting the burden of service to a smaller, self-selected cohort of citizens. The feeling seems to be that if they thank a military member or a veteran for their service, they have done their part in supporting the military. The comment, "Thank you for your service" has become almost patronizing in its use today.

The All-Volunteer Military has resulted in a wide inequity in sharing the cost of war, with a small percentage of American citizens who sacrifice more than their fair share. The general apathy that a vast multitude of Americans now have toward serving their country in the military has grown to proportions where national security is compromised and has caused an alarming increase in the civilian / military divide.

Ken Allard, a retired Army Colonel, military analyst, and author of national security issues, in his commentary entitled, *When Americans Won't Serve*, dated September 15, 2014, states that "Civic virtue is lost when other people's kids do all the fighting." He claims that we have become a nation so detached from the tradition of the American soldier-citizen established by our Founding Fathers, and a tradition they were proud of, that we now insist on fighting our wars using other peoples' kids.

Because the All-Volunteer Military is extremely expensive, both financially and socially, our leadership did not mobilize the nation after 9/11, but chose to fight the Global War on Terror using the National Guard and Reserve forces to supplement the active duty force when necessary. Col. Allard, in his commentary, asks the question, "Want to know why so many of those NCOs, Captains, and Majors have to serve three or four or more combat tours of duty?" He answers his question with the comment, "Got a mirror handy? Look in it and you'll have your answer." In 2014, when Col. Allard wrote his column, deploying a force to Afghanistan cost one million dollars per soldier per year.

One might ask, "Where is Congress in all this concern about the All-Volunteer Military?" After all, it is the Constitutional responsibility of Congress to raise Armies and maintain Navies for the national defense. Yet, we hear nothing about Congress being concerned or holding committee meetings in serious debate about this issue which has all the potential of becoming a national security crisis. I would imagine the reason for this is that members of Congress suspect that one way to immediately come under criticism from one's constituency, as well as a multitude of other citizens, which in turn means losing votes, would be to recommend a return to conscription and the draft. As I mentioned however, there are retired high-ranking military officers and retired high-ranking civilian defense officials who are expressing their concerns and recommendations.

Col. Allard identifies three West Pointers, all retired after distinguished military careers, who were bringing sustained, critical, attention to the once sacrosanct All-Volunteer Military Force. General Stanley McChrystal, who headed an Aspen Institute project aimed at producing a million-strong civilian service corps, says that "As Important as military service is during the individual's years of service, graduating military veterans into every part of American society upon completion of their military service, is absolutely critical. And we don't do that very well right now." This statement of General McChrystal is critically important and touches on what I consider to be the greatest loss to the nation resulting from an All-Volunteer Military Force, and which I will expound on later in this addendum.

Professor Andrew Bacevich of Boston University goes further, arguing in his book *Breach of Trust*, that the relationship between the armed forces and American society has been compromised when less than one percent of our citizens ever serve in uniform. Ambassador and retired Lt. Gen. Karl Ikenberry is even more critical when he argues that ending conscription has corrupted American civic virtue in his statement, "We collectively claim the need for robust armed forces…and yet as individuals we do not wish to be troubled or inconvenienced with any personal responsibility for manning the frontier."

Col. Allard, in his column, suggests establishing a tiered system of military service. Our expeditionary forces - Army, Navy, Air Force, and Marines - would remain the All-Volunteer Military Force, while the National Guard and Reserves could be increased through some form of conscription. Their mission, in addition to supplementing the All-Volunteer Force in times of increased manpower needs, could be expanded to meet other national security needs such as defending our notoriously porous southern border.

This suggestion of Col. Allard's concerning some form of conscription has been echoed by others. Alan Chase Cunningham, in his column entitled *Fifty Years Strong*, dated June 2023, also stated that many former Defense officials, including both commissioned General officers and high-level civilians, have advocated for a conscription system of some kind. Their rationale for bringing back a draft in some format goes beyond the political divide which exists, which includes both individuals from the political liberal left who think a draft would put an end to costly conflicts abroad by making it more difficult for the President to use our military for such conflicts due to public protest, and individuals from the political conservative right who consider a draft necessary for a stronger America to successfully wage war, if necessary, with potential enemies such as Russia, China, North Korea, and Iran.

However, the belief by the political left that a conscription system would limit "military adventurism" by limiting the President's tendency to commit combat troops abroad is questionable at best given previous experience. Actually, the All-Volunteer Force has in some respects caused Presidents to be more responsive to elected officials and American public opinion when deciding whether or not to commit American combat forces. Interventions in Libya and Syria were quickly curtailed by a backlash from elected officials and citizens against making large military commitments. Moreover, the President, when using the All-Volunteer Military for the Gulf War in 1991, the interventions in Somalia and Yugoslavia, and the initial large-scale deployments to Afghanistan and Iraq during the Global War on Terror, had to weigh those political and military decisions very carefully to gauge how Congress and the American public would react. In the above cases, the President had the support of the majority of Congress and the

American public, especially in the aftermath of 9/11. Thus, it would seem that although a conscription system might contribute to the President's need to carefully weigh the nation's response to his committing military forces abroad, it would seem that it is not a major factor in restricting a President's freedom of action to do so.

Nevertheless, historical events have shown that the All-Volunteer Military has, to some degree, made It easier for the decision makers to use the military option and put the military in harm's way without much in the way of consequences. Which brings up the question of whether, with the drastically reduced size of the All-Volunteer Military, it any longer has enough of a constituency to really matter when advising the President or Congress in such matters. Or when it comes to things like holding people accountable for their decisions.

For example, who should the American people hold accountable for a 20 yearlong war we decided to lose when we conducted an embarrassing, chaotic, and confused withdrawal of our military from Afghanistan, while leaving hundreds if not thousands of Afghan individuals who had assisted our forces in the war against terror to their own fate after we handed the country over to the Taliban, whom it was our initial mission objective to defeat and destroy when we first deployed our military into the country.

The political right advocates conscription and a return to a draft of some sort to build a stronger America to counter those nation-states with strong military forces and with whom there is strong potential that America will be at war in the future. It is important to remember that the Gates Commission, which initially established the All-Volunteer Military in 1973, foresaw this eventuality and the need for a mass increase in manpower to serve in times of such crisis. Although they considered the National Guard and Reserves critical in meeting this need, they also realized that, in an all-out war with a major power or combination of major powers, there would be a critical need for a stand-by draft which could promptly be put into effect for the mass wartime mobilization of large numbers of recruits.

This situation envisioned by the Gates Commission exists today. We are not presently at war with any major powers, but the potential for such war has never been higher. Concerning the National Guard and Reserve forces, they are no longer simply stop-gap or supplementary forces to the active military as the Gates Commission envisioned them to be and as they were originally designed to be. With the advent of the Global War on Terror, the length of the war, its increasing requirements, and the efforts of our military leaders to reduce the number of combat deployments for active duty individuals, the National Guard and Reserves were mobilized more and more and for longer and longer periods of time, and essentially became operational mission critical forces in conducting the war.

Therefore, since the All-Volunteer Military as it exists today will not have, in itself, the manpower necessary to fight an all-out war with one of, or a combination of, the major powers today, and that the National Guard and Reserve forces will be needed at the outset of hostilities, it is clear that the All-Volunteer Military, the National Guard, and the Reserve forces will go to war together. Thus, the only option for a mass mobilization of needed manpower, is conscription and a draft. It would be good to have a limited conscription system available at the onset of hostilities that could be rapidly expanded to meet recruitment needs. This is something our current military and civilian defense leaders must include in their planning for future defense needs.

Our military has had some form of conscription in place from the American Revolution to the Vietnam War. Some level of conscription, from minimal to heavy, was used in many of the U.S. conflicts; nevertheless, volunteerism was the dominant method of recruiting for much of the time, and as I mentioned before, it was a matter of pride for our Founders that the American military could be referred to as a citizens' militia. However, by the end of 2022, a recruiting crisis that was predicted by many became a critical mass, coinciding with the major concern that an astounding number of our younger population did not feel an obligation or duty to serve, nor see the value of military service.

The bottom line is simply this: As a nation, we are losing our ability to field a military force sufficient to accomplish the missions our political and military leaders assign them and maintain a fair distribution of number of deployments per individual, length of deployments, and number of unaccompanied tours of duty compared to accompanied tours of duty. Our options are either to curb these missions or find ways to both enable a moderate increase in our active duty forces when needed, and a major, rapid, building up of forces in the event of, God forbid, an all-out war with major nation-states.

When the Gates Commission established the All-Volunteer Military and left the door open for establishing a draft if needed, their goal was that active-duty volunteers could spend two years at home for every year served in a combat zone. For the National Guard and Reserves, the standard was set at six years at home for every year they were mobilized for overseas duty. This was later changed to four years at home for every year mobilized. However, with the draft never being reinstated during the twenty-year Global War on Terror, these rates could not be sustained, and the two years at home for every one year of combat duty for the All-Volunteer Force fell close to one year at home for every one year of combat duty. Additionally, for the National Guard and Reserve components, the four years at home for every one year mobilized for overseas combat duty fell to just over two years home for every year mobilized.

Given the lessons learned during the twenty year Global War on Terror, it should be clear to our civilian and military leaders that this country desperately needs innovative ideas and additional incentives to encourage our young men and women to fulfill their obligation for public service and particularly military service, along with a redesigned military to ensure timely access to the manpower needed to defend the nation during any scale of conflict, ranging from low intensity to moderate intensity to high intensity warfare.

And this brings me back to Col. (Ret) Ken Allard column which I referred to. His suggestion to reshape and increase the size and readiness of our National Guard and Reserve forces through some form of conscription makes sense. It would do two things: Provide a large, combat ready force immediately available to supplement the All-Volunteer Force, and it would provide an operating low-volume conscription system that could be rapidly expanded to meet a large increase in manpower needs in the event of all-out war. Additionally, as Col. Allard suggested, during peacetime this increased National Guard force could take on other missions such as defending our southern border, which is currently being overrun by multitudes of illegal immigrants.

And as far as encouraging our young men and women to meet their obligation for military service, his suggestion to link shorter terms of military service to earned educational benefits is a good start. My own suggestion would be to offer two years of college tuition plus other expenses for every year of military service.

A final word on conscription. Policymakers should keep in mind that conscription works most effectively when there is broad, bipartisan, public acceptance of a draft, such as in World War I and World War II, when it was clear that the nation's security and survival were at risk. If the public is convinced that national security is at stake, conscription will have broad support. This, in itself, should discourage any form of military adventurism on the part of political and military leaders.

The need for additional incentives for recruitment and some form of conscription to supplement the All-Volunteer Force is urgent. We must not repeat the situation where in the past individuals were called on to serve numerous repeated combat tours. We must, as Col. Allard pointed out, end the disgraceful dependence on "other people's kids" to fight our wars. We must end the corruption of American civic virtue which stems from the fact that less than 1% of our citizens ever serve in uniform, and the other 99% are given a free pass.

A speech given by President Joe Biden mentioned the fact that only 1% of our citizens defend the freedom of the other 99%. He spoke of it as something desirable, something to be praised, a major accomplishment to take credit for. I couldn't believe what I was hearing. My thoughts were: "Is this man, our Commander-in-Chief so obtuse, so uninformed, so devoid of wise reason and discernment, that he doesn't comprehend the fact that having only 1% of our population responsible for our defense is a gross violation of our tradition, our heritage, the values and vision of our Founding Fathers, and represents a clear and present danger to our nation, not to mention a total abandonment of common sense.

Does our Commander-in-Chief not realize that depending on only 1% of the population to defend the other 99% compromises the relationship between the armed forces and American society? Does he not realize that it enables a vast multitude of our young citizens to ignore any obligation to serve their country in the military and fail to see the value of that service to the nation and to themselves? Does he not realize that it forces a small percentage of American citizens to sacrifice more than their fair share, that it increases the civilian / military divide, and greatly decreases the equity and fairness of spreading the human cost of war across the society as a whole?

And for that matter, to carry this state of obtuseness even farther, does he not realize that the current Democrat policy of wokeism now infecting our military, with its transsexual components, gender changing components, and social engineering components is a sure road to disaster concerning our military's combat readiness. The military is not a proving ground for social engineering. It exists primarily to protect the nation against its enemies, and if war comes, to defeat those enemies and destroy their capability and break their will to continue hostilities, using whatever force necessary to accomplish it.

In his column, Col. Allard quoted Gen. Stanley McChrystal who I referred to before. I want to restate Gen. McChrystal's comment and then expand on it as the conclusion to this addendum, since I consider that his statement identifies the most serious and negative consequence which the establishment of the All-Volunteer Military has had on the nation as a whole.

Gen. McChrystal's statement was as follows: "As important as military service is during the individual's years of service, graduating military service alumni into every part of American society is critical. And we don't do that very well now." This statement of Gen. McChrystal is filled with meaning and must be understood by all our civilian and military leaders, as well as the general population.

The General is saying that the importance of people's military service does not end when they leave the military after serving their commitment. It remains just as important when, as civilians, they take those military qualities and character traits which shaped them as Soldiers, Sailors, Marines, Airman, Coast Guardsman, and which stay with them after their service, into every part of American Society. This large infusion of those traits into society is critical to our Democratic Republic, our American way of life, and the nation's strength, power, national well-being, and international influence. And as the General said, we aren't doing very well infusing those traits into society today. Which leads to the question, why not? And the answer is, Because of the greatly decreased size of the All-Volunteer Force and the fact that less than 1% of our citizens ever serve in uniform. Let me go on to explain why I consider this the most serious of the negative consequences the establishment of the All-Volunteer Military has had on the country.

According to data from the U.S. Census Bureau, the share of the U.S. population with military experience has greatly declined. In 1980, seven years after the draft ended, the share of U.S. adults who were veterans had fallen to about 18%. Since then, however, that share of veterans has fallen drastically to 6% in 2022. This corresponds with the decrease in active duty personnel from 3.0 million to about 1.3 million in today's All-Volunteer Military, comprising less than 1% of all U.S. adults.

Along with this drastic decrease in the number of veterans in the population, there has been a drastic decrease in the number of veterans serving in the U.S. Congress. An analysis of the 118th Congress, conducted after the 2022 congressional elections, showed that in the current Congress only 18% or 78 of the 435 House Representatives are veterans, and only 17% or 17 of the 100 Senators are veterans. This was down drastically from decades past, when in 1975, 81% or 81 of the 100 Senators were veterans, and in 1967 when 75% or 326 of the 435 House Representatives were veterans.

Over the next 30 years, the total veteran population is projected to steadily and persistently decrease. Lt. Col. Charles Faint USA (Ret) owner of the *Havok Journal*, states in an article dated October 30, 2023, that the small percentage of active duty personnel and the small percentage of veterans in the population, combined with the drastic decrease of veterans in Congress makes it unlikely that national-level decision makers will have any kind of real relationships with military personnel, and therefore more than likely that fewer and fewer of these decision makers, as well as fewer and fewer of the population overall will feel any connection to the military, and view the military more as a concept than something made of flesh and blood.

This drastic decrease of veterans in the ranks of our civilian government leaders gives meaning and substance to Col. Allard's suggestion in his column that candidates for the Presidency and Congressional leadership positions have military service of some kind on their resumes, thus giving some assurance that they have learned the life-shaping lessons best learned while young. I would add the Secretary of Defense to those requiring prior military service. We would still have civilian control over our military, which is a constitutional requirement for a democratic republic, but it would be civilian control based on first-hand knowledge and experience of the military. Of course, having military service as a prerequisite for the Presidency or Congressional leadership would require the approval of the President and Congress, so let's not hold our breath.

It is, or should be, a matter of the greatest concern that the vast decrease of veterans in the population and the Congress over the years, and the even greater decrease to be expected over future years if nothing is done to correct it, combined with a vast decrease in the core values associated with the military, will have an incalculable devastating effect on our culture, society, institutions, and every aspect of what was considered the American way of life, which at one time was the envy of the world.

Let's consider those core values which the military is so effective in instilling in its young recruits. I mentioned some of them in the narrative of this book. Military service provides the individual with training, work experience, and character traits highly valued by the vast majority of employers. When they take this training, work experience, and core values into civilian life, it benefits their hometown, their community, their state, and the nation overall. Here are just some of those training and core values.

1. **Leadership Training**: The American military places great emphasis on leadership training from the rank of private on up. The reason for this training is that, in a combat situation, the Officers and NCOs in charge may become casualties, and a lower ranking individual must be able to take charge. Therefore, knowing basic leadership principles is a must. In peacetime and wartime, good leadership involves setting the example, giving clear and appropriate orders and directions, inspiring others to strive for excellence, and maintaining good order and high morale in the organization. Is it any wonder why civilian employers prefer hiring veterans with these qualities, and what a tragedy it is that these qualities diminish when the number of veterans in society diminish?

2. **Accountability**: The military member is held thoroughly accountable for his own behavior and actions, and if in a leadership position, also answerable for his subordinates' behavior and actions.

3. **Responsibility**: The military person learns from his first day in boot camp that responsibility is not a choice or an option; it is mandatory and a way of life, and any failure of responsibility is not tolerated because of its potential disastrous consequences in both combat and peacetime operations. Talking about responsibility, how about a military aviator in his early twenties operating a multi-million-dollar jet on a variety of demanding missions, or a young 18 year old crew chief responsible for the maintenance and mission ready status of his assigned aircraft.

Or how about that aircraft carrier deck crew of 17- and 18-year-olds, under the supervision of a petty officer not much older, who are cinching up the jets for catapult launch, and in whose hands the pilots are literally placing their lives, because one mistake in harnessing that jet to the catapult results in disaster to both jet and pilot.

There are many, many similar situations in the military where the responsibility for the maintenance, upkeep, and operation of incredibly complicated and expensive equipment and the associated risks are placed in the hands of trained young individuals in their late teens and early twenties, a responsibility unmatched by any given to their peers in the civilian world.

4. **Ability to Get Along with and Work with All People**: Teamwork is absolutely critical to virtually all military activity. There is no tolerance for any form of discrimination. This teamwork

often creates a bond between team members that is unbreakable, and frequently lasts long after military service is completed. The military was the first to desegregate under President Truman, and today remains as the major organization that is faithful to the Rev. Dr. Martin Luther King's exhortation to "judge not on the basis of a person's skin color, but on the content of a person's character."

    5. **Ability to Work Under Pressure**: Given the mission of the Military, many of the numerous operations to support that mission are of very high intensity, and working under pressure is more the norm rather than the exception. Most individuals who have been in the military for awhile have become accustomed to it, and are able to remain calm, mission oriented and keeping the objective in mind while working toward a solution while under physical, mental, and emotional pressure.

    6. **Systematic Planning and Organization**: Most military activities, including training exercises and operational missions, require thorough and detailed strategic and tactical planning, management of personnel and resources, careful consideration of objectives, strengths and limitations, logistic schedules and time management, along with timely assessments and adjustments. All this comes under systematic planning and organization, which all officers and NCOs are trained in, a talent that is obviously valued by civilian businesses and corporations.

    7. **Ability to Conform to Rules and Structure**: The military individual is subject to many rules and regulations designed to avoid confusion and breakdown in discipline and provide a solid structure for unified and efficient operations.

    8. **Loyalty**: A major character trait of the military individual is loyalty - loyalty to his unit, his peers, his leaders, his branch of service, and his country. This loyalty, beyond any found in most civilian organizations, is special because it stems from common sacrifice.

    9. **Flexibility and Adaptability**: The flexibility to quickly adapt to conditions and circumstances is an important aspect of the majority of military training that one receives, especially in a combat unit. This includes departing from the original plan of operations if changing conditions and circumstances warrant it, and to adapt to those changing conditions rather than give blind obedience to a faulty strategy. In this regard, the words of Napoleon come to mind when he was asked to comment on the leadership qualities of his Marshals. I believe it was Marshal Ney of whom Napoleon said, "He has all the qualities of great leadership, except one." When asked what that was, Napoleon stated, "He doesn't know when to disobey!" Finally, concerning work habits, military members are known for completing the mission or project at hand in a timely, effective, and efficient manner. If that entails working long, long hours, so be it. Pride, enthusiasm, and perseverance shape the work habits of military personnel.

    10. **Security Clearances**: The majority of military personnel have security clearances at some level, and those working in highly sensitive specialties and with highly sensitive equipment hold security clearances at the top secret level and beyond. Also, exhaustive background checks are conducted before an individual is given a security clearance, and the higher the clearance, the more exhaustive the background check.

    11. **Self-Direction**: Understanding difficult and complex issues and solving problems on the spot without having to seek step-by-step guidance from above by one's supervisor is a common military trait. Also, knowing when to take personal responsibility for corrective action and when

to seek guidance and direction from one's supervisor is a part of an individual's training and indoctrination.

12. **Initiative:** Relates to all the above traits. The military places high value on individual initiative, and it is one of the most important areas addressed on the individual's performance evaluations. A major concern today expressed by many political, business, educational, and cultural leaders is that initiative seems to be a core value that so many of our younger population lack. Well, the military has a way of forcing a person to show initiative whether they want to or not, because not to do so has consequences they definitely don't want. Yes, they may gripe, complain, and bitch about it, but the amazing thing is that when they see the success that comes from initiative, they want more of it. And so, initiative that was lying dormant in them is suddenly growing into a powerful core value. Remember my account about the former gang members in the book narrative, and the effect that being forced by the Drill Instructors to show initiative and give their very best efforts had on them.

13. **Education**: The military is one of the best educated population groups. All enlisted members have at least a high-school diploma or a GED, and many have college associate or bachelor's degrees. All officers have at least a college bachelor's degree; a large majority have master's degrees, and a good share have their Doctorates.

14. **Quality Standards**: Quality Control is of the utmost importance in the military, and excellence is the standard. It cannot be otherwise because of the critical nature of the mission - national security - and the budgeted resources devoted to that mission. Because quality control is of the essence, it is vitally important that all communication be clear, concise, and thorough. Eloquence is inspiring and has its time and place, but in combat, plain-speaking takes priority over eloquence. One is reminded of a technique General Dwight Eisenhower, Supreme Commander of Allied Forces in Europe during World War II, is said to have used to insure against confusing communication. When presented with an operational plan developed by his staff officers, he would have them bring in a Private from a nearby unit, swear him to secrecy, give him the plan to read, and then tell them whether he understood it or not. If he said "yes," the plan was put into effect; if he said "No," the plan was returned to the staff to redo until it could be understood by the lowest ranking grunt soldier. After all, those were primarily the ones who would have to implement the plan, and success or failure would result from whether or not they understood it.

15. **Global Outlook**: The military member is kept informed of the world situation from a national security standpoint. This normally gives the military member an increased level of maturity over his/her civilian counterpart. Additionally, a vast number of military personnel have served tours of duty overseas in various locations around the world. This international experience has broadened their knowledge regarding customs, cultures, economies, and languages of other countries, and this too gives them a level of maturity and knowledge above that of many of their civilian peers.

16. **Specialized Training**: All military service personnel receive advanced training in their specialties. Military training in the technical, engineering, medical, administrative, security, and other specialties is considered some of the best available and is highly preferred by businesses and corporations. For example, the airlines' top preference in hiring pilots is former military pilots because they know these pilots are the best trained pilots in the world. It's the same with their

hiring aircraft mechanics and avionics specialists; their preference is former military because they know that these individuals have had the best training available in those specialties. Another example is our law enforcement profession. Former military police specialists are on the preferred hiring lists of police departments around the country.

One could go on and on listing core values that the military instills in those who have served. Now consider the fact that when the military member leaves the military, when his commitment is completed, he/she takes those core values into their civilian life, their community, their job, their social activities. Consider the monumental benefits to our country, our states, our cities, our communities, our society and culture when decades ago, 40, 50 or more percent of our young people had served in the military and brought those core values with them when they returned to civilian life. Then consider the monumental loss to our country, our states, our cities, our communities, our society and culture of those core values when for five decades in the past, since the establishment of the All-Volunteer Military, only 1% of the population, instead of 40, 50 or more percent, have served or are serving in the military, while 99% are free of any obligation to serve. Is it any wonder that only 9% of our young adult population feel any obligation to serve their country in the military when fewer and fewer of them have the example of a family member who has military experience, or a friend who is serving or a friend who has served. Finally, consider the fact that today only 18% of Senators, and only 17% of the members of the House of Representatives have served in the military, and the negative impact that has had on the overall quality of leadership in government.

Is it any wonder that, with the monumental loss of those core values to our society and culture over the past 50 years or so, the country is on the decline and experiencing a drastic reduction in moral and ethical standards in our government, educational, and cultural institutions, while many of our major cities are inundated with homeless people, rampant crime, decaying infrastructure, bankrupt economies, and too many political leaders whose primary loyalty is to their political party and a lust for power, rather than to the country and the common welfare of the citizens.

The country desperately needs a new infusion of the core values best exemplified by our military - honor, virtue, responsibility, loyalty, sacrifice, and the others listed above. In choosing one's priorities in life, one cannot do better than God, Family, and Country, for with such priorities one will have a life that is a blessing to oneself and to others, and a life that will leave a lasting legacy.

After our Founders adopted the Constitution they had so brilliantly and painstakingly developed, Benjamin Franklin, upon leaving the convention hall, was asked by a woman, "What have you given us, Mr. Franklin?" His response was, "A Democratic Republic, if you can keep it!" Mr. Franklin's words serve as both a reminder and a warning. A reminder that in a Democratic Republic, we the people elect our leaders, and we better be very careful to choose leaders of faith, virtue, honesty, humility, courage, and a willingness to sacrifice for the good of the country and the common welfare of its citizens.

President Ronald Reagan said that we, as a nation, are always within one generation of losing our Democratic Republic and our freedoms. In other words, every generation of leaders and citizens must renew, reinforce, and reemphasize the principles, standards, morals, and ethics which guided our Founders in building the United States of America.

And his words serve as a warning that if our leaders and we citizens ever turn away from the Judeo-Christian foundation upon which they built this nation, if we turn away from the moral and ethical code of conduct embodied in the Ten Commandments which they chose for the nation, if we fail to remove corruption in government and our public institutions when it becomes apparent, if we fail in our willingness to serve and sacrifice for the good of the nation and our fellow citizens, and finally, if we reject the core values which our Founding Fathers emphasized in their writings and speeches, then this Democratic Republic which God blessed us with through our Founders, this first and greatest experiment in history of government of the people, by the people, and for the people, will certainly fail and fall.

God save us from such monumental calamity.

www.ingramcontent.com/pod-product-compliance
Lightning Source LLC
Chambersburg PA
CBHW081428070526
44586CB00020B/2526